T0316569

Cambridge Elements ≡

Elements in Child Development
edited by
Marc H. Bornstein
National Institute of Child Health and Human Development, Bethesda
Institute for Fiscal Studies, London
UNICEF, New York City

THE CHILD'S ENVIRONMENT

Robert H. Bradley
Arizona State University

CAMBRIDGE
UNIVERSITY PRESS

CAMBRIDGE
UNIVERSITY PRESS

University Printing House, Cambridge CB2 8BS, United Kingdom

One Liberty Plaza, 20th Floor, New York, NY 10006, USA

477 Williamstown Road, Port Melbourne, VIC 3207, Australia

314–321, 3rd Floor, Plot 3, Splendor Forum, Jasola District Centre, New Delhi – 110025, India

79 Anson Road, #06–04/06, Singapore 079906

Cambridge University Press is part of the University of Cambridge.

It furthers the University's mission by disseminating knowledge in the pursuit of education, learning, and research at the highest international levels of excellence.

www.cambridge.org
Information on this title: www.cambridge.org/9781108791410
DOI: 10.1017/9781108866040

First published 2020

A catalogue record for this publication is available from the British Library.

ISBN 978-1-108-79141-0 Paperback
ISSN 2632-9948 (online)
ISSN 2632-993X (print)

The Child's Environment

Elements in Child Development

DOI: 10.1017/9781108866040
First published online: October 2020

Robert H. Bradley
Arizona State University

Author for correspondence: robert.bradley@asu.edu

Abstract: The focus of this Element is on the environment and how it is implicated in children's development. A very broad array of social and physical features connected to children's home life and to the neighborhoods where children live, including multiple aspects of parenting, housing characteristics, and the increased prevalence of media in daily life, are addressed. Attention is also given to the broader social, economic, and geographic contexts in which children live, such as neighborhood surroundings and conditions in less developed countries. There is a focus on how various aspects of the home context (e.g., crowding) and key parental characteristics, such as mental illness and substance abuse problems, affect the behavior of parents. Consideration is also given to how various forms of chaos and instability present challenges for parents and children and how those circumstances are implicated in both children's development and caregiver behavior.

Keywords: parenting, home environment, cumulative risk, child development

ISBNs: 9781108791410 (PB), 9781108866040 (OC)
ISSNs: 2632-9948 (online), ISSN 2632-993X (print)

Contents

1 Introduction

Where people spend their time matters. Human development (even basic survival) depends on the conditions present in the places where one lives (Wong & Candolin, 2015). Life in a remote mountain area, an upscale suburb, or a congested inner-city neighborhood differs greatly. Likewise, living alone with a single parent tends to be very different from living in a multigenerational household where several siblings are present. Because we humans are conscious of our surroundings, we are to some extent a different person in each of those places. That does not mean that the conditions present in a setting fully determine how we act. Each of us has a personality that helps determine our identity and guide our behavior. Even so, each individual's personality and motivational dispositions are to some degree transformed as a consequence of the places where that individual spends time. The focus of this Element is on the social and physical conditions connected with home life and how those conditions are implicated in children's development.

Where children spend time – including time in the womb – penetrates to every aspect of their being, down to their chromosomes (Boyce et al., 2013; Fernald & Maruska, 2012). How children spend time in various settings can change brain architecture and even how children's genes speak to one another (epigenesis) (Fox et al., 2010; Kundakovic & Champagne, 2014). Not surprisingly, research has shown that the environment has a major impact on children's overall development. In this regard, it is extraordinary to look back in time and to imagine how children have spent time throughout the course of history. The life of hunters and gatherers was remarkably different from the life of most children today, with even three-year-olds spending time on an iPhone and mom ordering dinner using an app downloaded from the Internet. The places where children spend time vary a great deal even today. Household residences range from tiny huts with no modern facilities to mansions where almost everything is controlled by apps on smartphones. Surrounding communities vary from sparsely populated areas with limited amenities to dense upscale urban neighborhoods with a multiplicity of eating, learning, shopping, recreational, and work establishments as well as multiple options for transportation.

There have been extensive changes in family life over the past hundred years, with technological changes being the most obvious. Yet there have been other changes as well: (1) family sizes have decreased, (2) more mothers work full-time, (3) there is less time spent with extended family, (4) children spend more time in formal education and less time in natural surroundings, (5) homes are bigger, (6) homes contain far more amenities and materials, and (7) human communities have become more densely populated and more diverse. For many children, there is remarkable instability in the social and physical accoutrements of daily life as they move from infancy and early childhood to adolescence and emerging adulthood (Seltzer, 2019). That said, life on earth today varies enormously. For example, the life of indigenous children in the Arctic only vaguely resembles the lives of native children in sub-Saharan Africa even today (Burnette & Figley, 2016; You & Anthony, 2012) – geography, like history with its technological advances, helps determine the way time is spent and what it means to someone.

A study using time-diary data collected from families across the United States showed how recent changes in family life can affect the ways children spend time and how this matters for children (Hsin & Felfe, 2014). When mothers worked full-time, they spent fewer hours per week in the presence of their children, most notably time in unstructured activities. Critically, more time spent in unstructured activity was related to both lower levels of child competence and higher levels of maladaptive behavior. Similar findings emerged in a nationwide study of Australian families (Craig et al., 2014). Working mothers spent less time overall with children. However, joint activity between working mothers and children was more active and child-centered. By contrast, paternal time providing direct care for children increased overall.

Children and parents are spending more time together at home nowadays, owing to the fact that children now spend more time inside the house than was true in the past (Mullan & Chatzitheochari, 2019). However, there has been almost no change in the amount of time children and parents are actually together at home. The increased presence of media devices has translated to parents and children (especially older children) spending more time in the same house together but not involved in joint activity.

Affordances of a setting are its functionally significant properties, considered in relation to a particular individual (Heft, 1993). An environmental affordance is something perceivable and psychologically meaningful to an individual. Accordingly, it can influence the individual's motivational dispositions (i.e., increase or decrease the likelihood an individual will engage in a particular action toward a psychologically meaningful goal). What is important to understand about environmental affordances is that they are not, in the deep sense, actual properties of the environment per se (Chemero, 2009). Rather, affordances pertain to the relations between features of a particular setting and the proclivities and capacities of a given individual. No two people "see" a setting in exactly the same way, nor do they see themselves as participants in a setting in the same way as others see themselves as participants in the same setting (Belanger & Coolen, 2014). For example, a stream may present quite different affordances for water play for a child living in the rural Midwest, United States than a child living in downtown New Delhi, India.

As phylogenetically advanced creatures, humans are designed to learn from, utilize, and help reconstruct the places they inhabit. Although theory and research make reasonably clear that humans reflect the conditions present in the places they inhabit (Heft, 2018), we are only beginning to figure out how the various features of children's contexts matter for various aspects of their development. In this treatment of the environment for children, an effort will be made to review what is known about how environments affect the well-being of children. The review will include information from diverse sources, including governmental reports, reports from international agencies, empirical studies, qualitative accounts, meta-analyses, literature reviews, and policy documents. The focus will be on various settings and features of the environment (particularly the home environment) and what is known about how those settings/features affect children's behavior and development and how they affect the behavior of adults who provide care for children (particularly parents). Attention will also be given to how relations between environment and development may evolve during the first decade of life. The review will begin with a consideration of several broad frameworks that seem useful in understanding children's environments: (1) the concept of human habitats, (2) the dynamic interplay of social and physical features in human settings, and (3) systems theories. Special consideration will be given to features of human habitats that seem especially relevant to children's development (i.e., the penetration of media into daily life and the broad urban/rural divide that affects life throughout the world). Special consideration will also be given to parenting processes that influence children's well-being and to contextual challenges that affect both children and parents.

2 Habitat

As increasing numbers of humans have moved into densely populated areas that vaguely resemble human habitats of the past, concerns have arisen regarding how well humans are adapting to the conditions present in such crowded places (Besson, 2017). Habitats, and the settings that compose them, vary in both their structural features and the kinds of interdependence that exist among the actors that dwell in them. The features of particular settings convey multiple messages to those who inhabit them, messages that evolve over time. No two people experience (or make use of) a given habitat in the same way (Belanger & Coolen, 2014). A young child is likely to "see" a place differently than an adult. A person of low social position is likely to see a place in a different manner than a person of power and wealth.

There are worries that the modern built environment often does not meet humans' instinctive needs, needs shaped by a lengthy evolutionary history. There are also worries about how people, children especially, perceive nature. Most ten- and eleven-year-old children living in a large urban city in the United States reported they had little experience of being in "natural settings" (Aaron & Witt, 2011). The children often equated "nature" with anything outside rather than limiting the concept of nature to settings that contained natural elements such as plants, trees, animals, and wild landscapes. Although most children felt that being in nature allowed them freedom to play, a number also expressed fears they might experience harm from wild things.

There is accumulating evidence that having "natural" elements in one's surroundings induces a sense of relaxation and well-being; and it increases one's proclivity to engage with objects and people (Dadvand et al., 2017; White et al., 2013). There is evidence that exposure to nature also increases brain volume (Dadvand et al., 2017, 2018). That said, the findings to date offer only limited support for the specific benefits derived from experience with nature (Stamps, 2004; Triguero-Mas et al., 2015). Interpreting findings is difficult because individual research projects have looked at quite diverse features of community environments (e.g., parks, indoor plants, access to forests), at quite diverse subpopulations, and at a multiplicity of outcomes using a diverse array of methodologic approaches (Hartig et al., 2014).

A factor that makes it particularly difficult to evaluate the "effects" of being in nature is that most studies have focused on short-term outcomes or processes (e.g., engaging in physical activity) that are presumed to drive longer-term outcomes (Hartig et al., 2014; Wheeler et al., 2010). Most research has not considered potential cofactors that may contribute to positive health outcomes (higher socioeconomic status [SES]; better air quality in places with more plant life; less crime and more social cohesion in neighborhoods that have more parks; greater access to recreational resources in addition to greater access to parks). Future research might focus on how particular features of habitats offer benefits to children and adults. An example would be to look at children's activities in settings that include elements from nature, with a view to determining how such elements impact various components of development (Cox et al., 2018).

When considering future research on how the features of settings promote or hinder child well-being, it might also be productive to look at features of current settings (e.g., residential dwellings, schools, neighborhoods, etc.) that seem antithetical to the needs of humans, based on how modern habitats tend to diverge from the habitats ancient humans experienced. Studies in this genre have already shown that living in high-density neighborhoods with limited access to parks and with low levels of vegetation reduces the amount of physical activity for children and increases the likelihood of obesity (Ding et al., 2011). That said, social scientists are struggling to identify methodologies that can accurately characterize the quality and suitability of particular environments as they pertain to specific goals for humans (Han et al., 2018).

3 The Dynamics of Human Settings

As children age, they do more to select and construct the settings where they spend time (Scarr & McCartney, 1983). In effect, older children do more to fashion the affordances of the places they inhabit. Kyatta (2002) argued that how a particular feature of the environment is engaged depends on what an individual brings to it, including the individual's personality, prior learning, and history of social experience. Kyatta connected the idea of setting affordances to ideas about different types of actions people take – specifically, free or spontaneous actions, promoted actions, and constrained actions. The latter two types of actions are often informed by culture or social networks, which may help establish the value or appropriateness of the actions. When circumstances change, such as when a family moves or a community provides new types of infrastructure, the affordances of particular environmental features may change as well.

One of the greatest challenges in understanding how the features of a setting influence the developmental course for children is that settings have many features; and their co-occurrence is not random. Key conditions, like crowding and noise (see Sections 7.1.2 and 7.1.3 on noise and crowding respectively), often co-occur since both are more often present in settings inhabited by marginalized groups, such as those living in poverty or in stigmatized communities. Accordingly, some of the "observed" impacts of one feature likely reflect the impacts of co-occurring features. Critically, even when researchers have thoughtfully controlled for family contextual circumstances when looking at relations between a particular condition (e.g., crowding, noise), they have not actually examined how the co-occurrence of particular conditions may be implicated in a particular developmental outcome. Knowing that noise and crowding are likely to co-occur is one thing; actually documenting how their co-occurrence in a real setting affects a particular outcome for a particular group of individuals is another. Consider, as an example, living in a crowded, noisy home with insufficient heat and with smoke from a wood-burning stove. This is even more likely to pose threats to well-being than just living in a crowded house or a noisy house or a house with internal smoke present. To better understand the influence of any of those conditions/affordances, one needs to take account of the other conditions and actually document their interplay.

Humans are complex creatures who react not simply to a particular feature in a setting but to the amalgam of conditions present. Thus, studies that look more deeply at the co-occurrence of two or more conditions both in and through time would seem useful in clarifying how any particular type of condition functions to affect the developmental course. Consider, as an example, the full set of social and physical features present in a home. A child who lives in a home with lots of games and learning materials, where parents spend time with the child in learning activities, and where there are good routines will likely have high learning motivation and good academic performance. There is likely to be co-occurrence of the three conditions, but co-occurrence is not inevitable; so, to understand how each condition functions to affect a child's motivational tendencies and competence, it would be useful to examine the interplay. Controlling for SES provides only a hint of how each condition works. Efforts in the direction of looking at multiple conditions in a habitat simultaneously have been made in studies of neighborhood conditions that facilitate children's outdoor play. Studies have included such things as traffic flow, availability of parks, amenities in nearby playgrounds, walkability of the neighborhood, and so on – albeit rarely have all such conditions been considered in the same study (Aziz & Said, 2012).

Looking at multiple features of human habitats to determine how those features function to affect human behavior, useful as it is, is still not enough. People are conscious actors; and how they feel about a place makes a difference in how they respond to its features. Scannell and Clifford (2017) make a strong case for how place attachment (to home, neighborhood, community, country) plays a role in how people feel about their surroundings and themselves. A strong sense of bonding with place appears to have a number of psychological benefits, including a more positive feeling about one's overall quality of life. In contrast to research showing that living in a space perceived as crowded increase one's stress, strong bonding to a place leads to a state of relaxation for children as well as adults (Korpela et al., 2002). That said, relatively little is known about the "benefits" of place attachment in children.

At present, there is limited knowledge about how children perceive the affordances of most settings, with research often addressing children in certain age groups only, children in certain cultural groups, and children from certain geographic locales. There have been a few studies that have focused on how children perceive their "home range" (i.e., the area around a child's residence where they spend time independent of an accompanying adult). A study of nine- to eleven-year-old children who attended schools in three urban centers in New Zealand revealed that the size of a child's home range varied a great deal, with boys stating they had somewhat larger home ranges than girls – albeit not by much – and they were larger if the child had friends nearby (Hand et al., 2018). As expected, children with more restrictive parents and children who lived in neighborhoods with more traffic had smaller home ranges. Not surprisingly, because the children lived in urban areas, very few had home ranges that included woodlands and other natural habitats. As a consequence, the children's experiences and engagement with nature mostly involved time spent in home gardens and nearby parks rather than "wild nature."

Given that perceptions about environmental affordances involve the interplay of multiple personal and contextual conditions, the dearth of knowledge makes it difficult to draw strong conclusions about what matters with respect to the features of settings and how they matter. It would be useful if future research concentrated on how various sensory features of settings promoted positive motivational tendencies and enabled the development of various types of skills. It would also be useful if future research concentrated on social features of settings, particularly interpersonal interactions and group behavior in particular types of settings and how those behaviors promoted positive motivational tendencies. Increased knowledge in these areas would facilitate training for caregivers and for designing more productive settings for children.

4 Systems Theories

Humans are self-organizing creatures, with a multitude of skills and proclivities, which allows an outflow of approaches to engaging environments (Lewis, 2000). A preschooler may suddenly grab plush toys from the toy box and create an animal park where they are the zookeeper. A teen may join a social media platform, then send selfies to unknown others, hoping to gain "followers." For every individual, there is an ongoing emergence of new understandings of what a setting might afford, new activities to consider, and new identities to reflect on. In the process, things once seen as meaning very little can suddenly mean a lot. Given the complex nature of self-organization, the meaning of interplay between person and environment can be difficult to determine with precision. Over the past three-quarters of a century, a number of theories aimed at explaining the complex interplay of humans and their environments have emerged, theories that view humans as members of dynamic, constantly evolving systems involving people, places, and things. The focus of this section is to overview several systems theories and their potential applicability in understanding how children engage with their environments and are shaped by those environments.

Most systems theories that are used to explain human behavior as it relates to environmental conditions derive from general systems theory. Two basic postulates from general systems theory help make clear why humans have such diverse responses to their environments: (1) multifinality – the idea that the same condition can lead to different outcomes or end states; and (2) equifinality – the idea that different conditions can lead to the same outcome or end states (Von Bertalanffy, 1968). The implications of these two basic principles of general systems theory will be seen repeatedly in Section 6 on caregiving processes associated with child well-being (e.g., certain risk factors can lead to a multiplicity of different parenting problems, and different risk factors can lead to the same parenting problem).

The broad literature on human systems makes clear that a given setting does not afford the same opportunities for exploration for all those who encounter it (Wachs, 2000). It is also the case that not everyone in a given environmental setting has an equal level of desire or wherewithal to exploit the affordances the setting provides. The organization of materials or the pace of action within a setting (or niche) may privilege some inhabitants more than others, as may social expectations and constraints (Raymond et al., 2017).

Ecological-developmental theories depict human beings as self-stabilizing. According to dynamic systems theory, individual behavior patterns tend to become organized around a small number of "attractors" (i.e., functionally connected ideas and behaviors that exert mutual control on each other). These attractors tend to be reasonably stable through time (Lewis, 2000). A habitat with consistent patterns of social and physical features will promote an individual's behavioral tendencies and maintain the individual's expectations as regards oneself and one's goal pursuits. However, if conditions change, it may disrupt patterns of behavior, moving the individual toward withdrawal or behavioral adaptation. Changes in behavior are likely when children experience trauma or family dissolution (De Bellis & Zisk, 2014; Hetherington & Stanley-Hagan, 1999; Laursen et al., 2019). Dramatic changes in home life (or broader conditions) can reduce the power of positive skills and dispositions to help children manage the new conditions. As it happens, relations between a particular risk condition and children's behavior are often nonlinear, with research showing different impacts for different children and variations in how long a particular outcome persists (American Psychological Association, 2008; Runyan et al., 2002). It also depends on what happens after the disruptive event occurs (Lamela & Figueiredo, 2016).

The features present in a child's life are not likely to show a linear relation with most developmental outcomes (e.g., having 500 children's books in a child's home is not likely to build the child's vocabulary that much more than having 100 children's books). According to Holland (1992), complex adaptive systems form and use internal models to anticipate the future, basing their actions on an assessment of the affordances present in any circumstance and their anticipation of expected outcomes. Humans are governed systems that operate in accordance with rules. Among the properties that determine how an individual will respond to contextual opportunities and constraints is nonlinearity; that is, different features of the settings that humans encounter become more or less ascendant as humans evolve and get more experience. As a consequence, the "rules" that govern interactions between a person and particular features of the environment are constantly evolving; and they help determine how the person develops. Holland contended that humans, as complex adaptive systems, engage in "a kaleidoscopic array of simultaneous interactions" (p. 19) with other systems. Thus, individuals need to adjust their beliefs and behaviors in ways that help them adapt to the conditions present in their environments. However, humans vary in their ability to reorganize their ideas and behaviors to meet the challenges and expectations present in the places they inhabit – with young children being particularly vulnerable in this regard. In vulnerable systems, even small disruptions can have fairly dramatic consequences. If the environment does not contain a sufficient number of supportive features or if it is unstable, it can be difficult for an individual to reorganize in ways that are productive for even short-term well-being (Folke, 2006).

When considering how features of settings where children spend time affect learning and development, it is critical to bear in mind that humans are composed of numerous developmental subsystems that are mutually influential. Cunha and Heckman (2007) provide evidence that various skills (a term that includes health, adaptive functioning, motivational proclivities, and competence) operate in complementary ways to increase overall skill development (or well-being more generally) – what they refer to as dynamic complementarity. The central argument is that strengths in one area of skill (e.g., cognitive competence) can help support the development of strength in another area of skill (e.g., adaptive coping). As a consequence of this process, children are likely to benefit most when their environments offer supports for multiple skills because development in each area of skill helps promote development in other skill areas. Likewise, when an environment does not offer supports for a particular skill area, more is left to the individual to compensate for the lack of support in a given area and greater is the likelihood that there will be less development in multiple skill areas. A second implication of the idea of dynamic complementarity is that, when one component of a child's overall environment (e.g., the family) does not provide adequate support for skill development, the child will become more dependent on a second component of their overall environment (e.g., the school).

Sociocultural theory (Rogoff & Morelli, 1989) speaks to how children develop competencies and motivational tendencies pertaining to particular types of activities. Central to the theory is that competence development depends on the quality of mutual exchanges between a child and those who are more knowledgeable (most often adults) and on the nature of the objects and arrangements present in those exchanges. Highly productive "guided participation" results when adults offer interpersonal supports and carefully targeted challenges to a child. It can be difficult for young children to comprehend what is required in unfamiliar settings or when encountering unfamiliar people; thus, they may struggle to productively engage with the people and things in unfamiliar territory. Prior experience in a multitude of settings, under the guidance of caregivers who help children appraise situations carefully (i.e., promote key cognitive skills) and act with thoughtfulness and confidence (i.e., promote key motivational skills), can lead to the development of productive social and emotional skills (Goldstein & Lerner, 2018).

Because humans are complex adaptive systems engaged in ongoing interplay with complex environments, it is difficult to construct a theory that adequately explains why any given person behaves the way they do or precisely predicts an individual's developmental course. What seems clear, however, is that children need well-structured, manageable, and sustained exchanges with people and objects in their immediate surroundings. Otherwise, they experience stress and fatigue, which leads to withdrawal or negative patterns of behavior. Children also need the skills to cope with whatever challenges their surroundings present and that allow them to construct supportive life niches (Prilleltensky et al., 2001; Repetti et al., 2011). Even when children generally have the skills to manage the challenges present in the settings where they spend time, changes in their skills and in their environments lead to constant renegotiation with the physical and social elements present in those settings aimed at a good (aka adaptive) fit (Neufeld et al., 2006). As Holland (1992) would say, it is an ongoing rule discovery procedure, a procedure that is critically informed by the actual affordances present in the environment *in* and *through* time. Despite the limitations in theory and research as applied to person–environment interplay and how it impacts developmental course, what does seem reasonably clear is that optimal fit between person and environment can only occur when the affordances of the environment allow for the realization of basic human needs and the development of multiple types of targeted, complementary skills

(Cuhna & Heckman, 2007; Fischer, 1980; Ryan & Deci, 2017). Research aimed at delineating critical connections between various types of needs and skills should help set the groundwork for successful parenting and educational activities as technology changes the landscape of human activity.

5 Features of Today's Habitats and the Cultures They Create

The places where people live now tend to be remarkably different from the kinds of places humans inhabited in the past. Until recently most humans lived in small residential facilities. Their "homes" were in natural surroundings and contained few amenities. Nowadays homes are more spacious, more complex, and they are more tightly intertwined with other man-made environments. This is less so for homes in poor countries, but even in poor countries fewer residences connect to natural surroundings (Bradley, 2012). While at home, increasing numbers of children spend less time with others and nature and more time with commercially constructed objects, such as smartphones or internet-enabled devices (Johnson, 2010). These differences insinuate themselves into how children think, what they value, and how they form identities.

Attitudes and beliefs evolve to accommodate changes in the environment. They are, in one sense, lagging indicators pertaining to the meaning of place. Changes in life over the past two centuries have been so far-reaching that societies have not come to terms with their significance and parents have not determined how best to rear offspring. Nowadays people tend to be more mobile. They change jobs, schools, childcare arrangements, and move to new locales. Higher mobility, together with changes in the physical trappings of life, contributes to diversity in lifestyles and openness to what life represents. This is changing the nature of interpersonal relationships; and it is changing where family members look for guidance in planning activities and evaluating information. Critically, it is changing parent–child relationships. Whereas in the past adults were more expert in how to manage objects and events, there are now increasing instances of children becoming their parents' teachers or co-directors as regards social activities. The most obvious example, perhaps, is that children are becoming more adept in using new social media platforms and more adept at using multiplayer games on the Internet.

Research provides inadequate guidance on how best to thrive in today's world. What seems clear is that the rapid evolution in human environments requires constant coping and reorganization (Rice, 2012), some of which might be facilitated by access to materials and equipment now available in many homes. However, as predicted by dynamic systems theory, some changes in the conditions connected to home life may lead to major shifts in how families organize daily life and what parents value in caring for children. The strengths of systems theories and theories of human motivation notwithstanding, it isn't clear that current theory is fully up to the challenge of explaining relations between the conditions present in current human habitats and children's development. Thus, extensions of current theory to more precisely address emerging aspects of housing and the physical environment, like the one advocated by Johnson (2010), may be needed to guide productive research and personal agenda. Children's environments now present conditions that require more dexterity and precision in the information provided by developmental science if children are to engage in more productive life pathways.

5.1 The Multimedia Universe

Recent studies make evident that children, particularly children in high-income countries, are spending several hours every day engaged with media (Rideout, 2017; Strasburger et al. 2012). Research shows that 98 percent of all US children under the age of nine live in homes with a TV and some type of mobile device (Rideout, 2017). Having access to various forms of media affords new opportunities for learning, recreation, and social networking. For example, infants and toddlers can productively engage with grandparents and other relatives using video calls (McClure et al., 2018). Even so, some have voiced concerns that children can be exploited and suffer consequences with respect to their well-being when using such devices (American College of Pediatricians, 2016; Brooks-Gunn & Donahue, 2008). Preschool-age children who spend more than the time recommended by the American Academy of Pediatrics using media have lower levels of microstructural organization and myelination of brain white matter (Hutton et al., 2020).

Best estimates are that on a typical day more than 80 percent of children under six use some type of screen media and they spend about two hours doing so. In about one-third of homes, the TV is on most of the time. More critically perhaps, only about half of elementary school children adhere to guidelines for TV watching established by the American Academy of Pediatrics (< 2 hours per day) (Fakhouri et al., 2013). About half of preschool-age children have some type of console video game player available to them in the home. The majority of American homes have two or more TVs, with many children having TVs in their own rooms, with time spent with media greater in low-income homes (Rideout, 2017). Nearly nine out of every ten school-age children in the United States have access to a computer at home, and three out of four have internet access. Takeuchi (2011) reported that more than half of US American children routinely use some type of handheld gaming device and more than two-thirds play with TV-based video game consoles. Studies done in other high-income countries reveal similar patterns (Hardy et al., 2006).

Although there are still economic and urban/rural digital divides as regards access to particular media, the divide is less than was the case a decade ago (Perrin, 2019; Rideout, 2017). The generally high accessibility of media for children and a lenient attitude of parents toward media use convert to more average hours of access to media in the household (Roberts et al., 2005). When parents are frequent users of media, it increases the likelihood that children and parents will spend time together using some form of media for learning (Rideout & Katz, 2016).

For most of the time that preschool-age children spend watching TV, using computers, and playing video games, they do it independent of their parents (Takeuchi, 2011). This can be a problem, especially since young children do not readily learn from media as a consequence of their need to interact with real people to grow cognitively and linguistically (Kirkorian et al., 2008). Young children have limited memory capacity, symbolic thinking skills, and sustained attention; thus, they can struggle to understand what is presented on TV programs or videos (Barr, 2013; DeLoache et al., 2010; Richert et al., 2010). Part of the "video deficit" associated with screen time for young children is correctable if parents, siblings, teachers, and others prepare very young children for encounters with media by helping children understand the contingent nature of the images (Lauricella et al., 2010). Unfortunately, even when parents are present during times a child is engaged with video media, it does not necessarily mean that parents are carefully monitoring the content to assure it is age-appropriate (Rideout et al., 2006).

The evolving media landscape makes it difficult to evaluate how time spent with media affects children and parents. Parenting has evolved due to the penetration of media into life. Raines and Robinson (2018) found that 61 percent of new mothers believe internet-connected devices are the best way to promote child well-being. Part of the challenge in understanding the impact of media on children and parents derives from the diversity in media use (NPD Group, 2009; Rideout & Katz, 2016). Additional challenges derive from the fact that children of different ages use media in somewhat different ways and respond to aspects of media differently.

As children age, different aspects of media become more salient and children become more discriminating in their use of media (Chassiakos et al., 2016). During early childhood, children are able to benefit from educational media productions and access to computers at home, with low-income children appearing to derive particular benefit (Fish et al., 2008; Hurwitz, 2019). That said, there is evidence that more than two hours of daily exposure to media may result in lower achievement (American College of Pediatricians, 2016). As Schmidt and Vandewater (2008) noted, the "effects" of media consumption depend on whether the content is educational or entertainment in focus. However, there is no compelling evidence that exposure to such programming is generally better than exposure to more traditional forms of learning. Part of the inconsistency in patterns of results obtained thus far appears to reflect differences in the nature of media-based learning experiences that students are exposed to (Warschauer & Matuchniak, 2010). Critically, web-based instruction is a rapidly evolving component of the total media landscape for children – a type of meso-system phenomenon with little available research to indicate precisely what it portends for children's development.

Video games, tablets and smartphones, and some websites present experiences with quite different affordances than do TV, radio, and more traditional media; that is, they are interactive. They have features that are more like play. Thus, time spent using newer forms of media has the potential to assist children's development (particularly cognitive development) in ways similar to well-designed play experiences (Bavelier et al., 2010; Blumberg et al., 2019; De Lisi & Wolford, 2002; Lieberman et al., 2009). As games and activities on media devices have become more and more like those available in natural and educational settings, recommendations and standards pertaining to quality are emerging to help guide in the production of games that afford children positive learning and recreational experiences. Even so, there remain concerns about the sedentary nature of many such experiences (Lieberman et al., 2009).

Time spent using media affects how much time children spend in other activities (Vandewater & Lee, 2009). When children have electronic games, it reduces physical activity and increases BMI, especially for boys (Fakhouri et al., 2013; Salmon et al., 2005; Timperio et al., 2008). McHale and colleagues (2009) highlighted the point that children's engagement with media plays an important role in identity development, social networking, and connecting children to social institutions. On the downside, research indicates that watching media can contribute to children's fears and anxieties, with young children being particularly at risk due to their limited capacities to regulate emotions (James et al., 2017; Wilson, 2008). Social media and texting have become an integral form of communication between children and adults and between children and their peers (O'Keefe et al., 2011). However, there is increasing concern that extensive use of social media may have negative consequences for parent–child relationships, especially for older children (Mesch, 2006).

A meta-analysis indicated a modest association between viewing prosocial content on media and prosocial behavior in children (Mares & Woodard,

2005). However, the specific impact on children depends on what parents do to mediate children's use of media (Barkin et al., 2006). How parents mediate the use of media tends to reflect their broader style of parenting, with differences emerging as a consequence of parent education and culture (Livingstone et al., 2015). Mediation is more active with young children, moving to more co-use and restrictive forms as children get older (Coyne et al., 2017). There is evidence that active mediation on the part of others partially determines how children respond to media images (Nathanson & Cantor, 2000). For that reason, parental monitoring of children's media involvement can be instrumental in how media affects children's well-being; but monitoring can become increasingly difficult as children age (Livingstone & Helsper, 2008; Rideout et al., 2006).

Much remains unclear about transfer of learning across media and from media to other aspects of life (Wartella et al., 2009). Research on the effects of media exposure is challenged by confounds that exist between the overall amount of exposure to media children receive and the content present in those exposures. It is also challenged by confounds that exist between amount of exposure and other factors present in a child's social context, including parental and peer mediation of exposures (Oakes, 2009). A study of screen media activity and brain structure in youth points to the complexities of trying to determine how time spent with various sorts of media impacts children's development (Paulus et al., 2019). The study showed that screen media activity had impacts on brain structures that increased externalizing behavior but no impact on other brain structures that increased externalizing behavior; and it found inconsistent support that screen media activity had impacts on brain structures that support cognitive functioning.

Electronic media have become deeply insinuated into modern home life. By their nature, different types of media help guide the arrangement of objects and materials within the residence and influence the arrangement of space. Media within the home often drive the use of time and the structure of family activities. For this reason, Johnson (2010) argued for the inclusion of the techno-subsystem into Bronfenbrenner's ecological-developmental model. In support of the idea, he compared the amount of variance in language and cognitive development accounted for by internet use and family SES and found that the former accounts for a greater proportion of variance than the latter. Interesting as the comparison is, it is a bit misleading in that indices of other recreational and learning materials present in the home also account for more variance in child achievement than SES. Nonetheless, the idea that electronic media function as a meaningful subsystem of the home physical environment would appear to have merit.

5.2 The Urban/Rural Divide

The year 2007 marked a watershed in human history. For the first time, more people lived in urban areas than in small towns and rural areas (Ritchie & Rosser, 2019b; United Nations, 2019). It is estimated that, by 2050, two-thirds of all humans will live in urban areas. Living in a modern urban environment, especially a densely populated urban environment, offers a dramatically different set of affordances for children and adults than was commonplace even half a century ago. Migration from both inside and outside the country has left rural areas in the United States disproportionately populated by older adults and urban areas more racially and ethnically diverse (Pew Research Center, 2018). As it happens, some geographic areas are rich in the kinds of resources required to support children's needs for competence, relatedness, and autonomy as well as to promote and sustain their health (Ryan & Deci, 2017). When one's place of residence offers an array of positive features, it is likely to inculcate a sense of place attachment (Morgan, 2010) as well as a sense of well-being, belongingness, and enjoyment (Lewicka, 2011; Scannell & Gifford, 2017). By contrast, when the geographic areas where children reside do not afford the resources and structures that allow children to engage intrinsic motivations, they will likely contribute to lower self-regulation and competence, poorer behavioral adjustment, and a sense of alienation. Not surprisingly, there tends to be substantial differences in the amenities and opportunities present in rural and urban areas generally, differences that can help determine the developmental trajectories of children (Bradley, 2012). In this section, attention is given to some of the differences research suggests might be particularly important for child well-being.

Scholars generally divide areas of residence into three broad categories: rural, urban, and suburban (Pew Research Center, 2018). Greater wealth accumulation and higher living standards are more prevalent in the latter two (Ritchie & Rosser, 2019b). However, both urban and rural environments sometimes contain "slums" (i.e., areas that have few amenities and limited upkeep; Housing Assistance Council, 2012). The percentage of substandard houses is a little higher in rural areas than in metropolitan areas (Housing Assistance Council, 2012).

Perceptions about places devolve from both cultural constructions and realistic appraisals about what these environments afford (Nairn et al., 2003). A number of factors affect people's sense of community and level of involvement within the community, including individual perceptions of how safe the area is and how secure they feel about the income they have (Funk et al., 2007). Rates of injury, death, and suicide in rural areas exceed rates of injury, death, and suicide in urban and suburban areas in the United States (Fontanella et al., 2015; Meyers et al., 2013; Nestadt et al., 2017). Increasing rates of suicide in rural areas have also been observed in Europe (Middleton et al., 2003). With all the changes that are occurring in rural, suburban, and rural areas in the United States, it is notable that less than 20 percent of residents in urban, rural, and suburban areas feel strongly attached to their community even though a substantially higher percentage of rural residents know their neighbors and believe that other members of the community share their values (Pew Research Center, 2018). Findings in the Pew report also make clear that there are racial/ethnic divides in both suburban and rural areas with respect to how adults perceive the problems they face. In both types of communities, ethnic minorities believe they face substantially more difficulties. To some extent, findings in the United States mirror findings obtained in other technologically advanced countries. However, the limited research on populations in less affluent countries tells a somewhat different story. Because of deteriorating economic conditions in most rural areas in less affluent countries, those living in rural areas generally report less life satisfaction than those living in more urban areas, even given the congestion and pollution often found in dense urban environments in many countries (Easterlin et al., 2011).

Living in a rural area often means that families have to travel longer distances to access various types of support services (Pearce et al., 2012). Data show that rural families in the United States are less likely to have ready availability of center-based childcare and preschool (Henly & Adams, 2018). The shortfall in licensed childcare and early education facilities may partially account for the lower scores on measures of school readiness shown by children living in rural areas; albeit the latter finding may also reflect that a high percentage of families living in rural areas are poor and that rural parents tend to be less well educated. That said, children from rural areas have reasonable access to public schools, and states have increasingly funded pre-kindergarten programs in rural areas. Access to pre-K and public schools in rural areas appear generally sufficient given recent studies on student achievement. More specifically, findings pertaining to eighth-grade exams from the 2011 National Assessment of Educational Progress showed that a lower percentage of rural students scored "proficient" than suburban students; however, a higher percentage of rural students scored "proficient" than was the case for eighth-grade students from concentrated urban areas or small towns. Nonetheless, there continues to be an urban/rural divide with respect to access to education in many countries, with research showing negative impacts on rural children's achievement (van Fleet et al., 2012; Zhang et al., 2015).

Rural families are less likely to have easy access to healthcare, particularly specialists important for prenatal care and serious illnesses and injuries (US Department of Health and Human Services, 2017). As it happens, mortality rates for young children are higher in rural areas and children with special healthcare needs are less likely to be seen by a pediatrician (Healthy People 2020, 2019; Iezzoni et al., 2006; Skinner & Slifkin, 2007). Indeed, it is not unusual for rural parents who have a child with a severe disability or a major healthcare need to relocate to a more populated area where advanced healthcare services are available. Access to services for behavioral healthcare also tends to be more limited in rural areas (Hauenstein, 2008; Semansky et al., 2012). Finally, children living in rural areas where pesticides and herbicides are used to improve crop yield and children living in areas near mines can also be at high risk for exposure to teratogens that lead to health problems (Jaishankar et al., 2014).

Living in an urban or suburban area often affords children more opportunities for potentially enriching activities, such as libraries and museums (Real & Rose, 2017). Those living in rural areas (especially remote areas) also tend to have less access to the Internet and other media (Perrin, 2019). By contrast, living in more densely populated areas may increase the likelihood of stress-producing social interactions and challenging events. Growing up in an urban environment can have a negative impact on amygdala activity and on perigenual anterior cingulate cortex activity, a major stress-regulation system (Lederbogen et al., 2011).

It appears that living in an urban environment increases the level of social stress. Important to consider, however, is that the greatest proportion of adults with psychiatric problems live in deprived inner-city neighborhoods and not in more advantaged urban neighborhoods. Moreover, some of the concentration of those with psychiatric problems in poor urban areas appears to reflect selective migration into urban areas rather than stress exposure from living in those areas. Critically, the rates of mental, behavioral, and developmental disorders are higher in rural communities, as is the incidence of child maltreatment (Meit et al., 2014; US Department of Health and Human Services, 2019). Overall, children living in rural areas are more likely to experience adverse childhood experiences than is the case for their urban counterparts (Crouch et al., 2019). However, figures favoring rural or urban households with respect to most adverse outcomes for children at least partially reflect household income and whether the parents abuse substances.

Life in remote rural areas tends to be very different from life in densely populated urban areas, and both tend to be different from life in upscale suburban areas. That said, there is substantial variation within each of these contexts, partly owing to age, socioeconomic status, nativity, country of residence, and ethnicity. Critically, much remains undocumented about how both children and adults spend their time and whether there tends to be different patterns of parent–child interaction in the urban, rural, and suburban environments. One of the few studies that directly compared parenting in rural and urban areas found that rural parents were somewhat less warm and responsive when caring for their children; and they were also less stimulating, even when controlling for race/ethnicity, maternal education, maternal depression, household income, and marital status (Miller & Vortruba-Drzal, 2013). The study also found that rural parents seemed to have less knowledge about child development and lower expectations for their children's achievement. Substantial research needs to be done quickly on how life in urban, rural, and suburban areas is affecting the lives of families, given the rapid advances in technology and rather quickly shifting demographics in each of the areas.

As Section 7.5 on lower- and middle-income countries (LMICs) makes clear, those who live in rural areas in LMICs tend to face substantial hardship, as there tends to be multiple structural constraints to their health and limited opportunities to acquire needed capabilities (Strasser, 2003). Families living in rural areas in many LMICs lack access to basic resources such as sanitation facilities, electricity, healthcare, education, and improved drinking water (Nandy & Gordon, 2009; UNESCO, 2010; UNICEF, 2019).

As stated at the beginning of Section 5, human habitats and the affordances present in many human settings have changed dramatically over time. Throughout the course of history, humans have attempted to fashion new tools to fit their environmental conditions and to improve life in those conditions. As a consequence, life prospects for many humans has improved – increased life expectancy being a noteworthy illustration of human progress (Roser et al., 2019). In some ways, efforts to save extremely preterm infants represent the essence of environmental intervention into people's lives. Extraordinary measures are taken to assist the children in managing such basic processes as breathing. Major advances have been made over the past century, advances that involve not only high levels of personal care by health professionals but also the use of advanced technologies. Even so, impact on the lives of most extremely preterm children has been limited (Brumbaugh et al., 2019). There is now widespread belief that robots and smart technologies will change almost everything about human life in the near future; but with uncertainties as to how those changes will impact the nature of social relationships and the meaning of life itself (Rossiter, 2017). Significant changes could occur in parent–child relationships, especially if chromosomal changes are made in human embryos – "I don't see me in you."

6 Caregiving Processes Associated with Child Well-Being

Because humans are so complex and take so long to reach maturity, they require a diverse array of supports from the environment in order to thrive, supports that change in form as they move from infancy to adulthood. Many of these supports are provided by caregivers. Accordingly, I developed a heuristic framework for organizing the key tasks of caregiving that parents (and other caregivers) need to provide children (Bradley, 2006). Central to the framework is the notion that optimal caregiving (a facilitative home environment) is best understood as a set of regulatory acts and conditions aimed at helping children successfully adapt to the conditions present in the settings they inhabit and successfully exploit the resources those settings contain. The framework is consistent with the idea that humans consciously engage with their environments and with the idea that maximum adaptation entails building personal assets over an extended period of time (Ford & Lerner, 1992; Lewis, 2000; Scales & Leffert, 1999). The framework for caregiving includes seven primary tasks that parents (or other caregivers) need to perform on behalf of children. I refer to them as the "7 Ss of Effective Caregiving": (1) provide *sustenance*, (2) assure *safety*, (3) provide *stimulation*, (4) generate *socioemotional support*, (5) engage in *surveillance*, (6) provide *structure*, and (7) facilitate *social integration*.

As stated, the "7 Ss" framework is a heuristic approach aimed at helping organize a very extensive literature on various types of parenting actions that theory and research suggest are important to children's development. In this section, research pertaining to each component of the caregiving framework is described. There is a focus on how each task of caregiving is implicated in children's development and how each is influenced by caregiver characteristics and contextual circumstances.

6.1 Sustenance

Children have many component psychobiological subsystems that require years to reach full maturity. Therefore, it is critical that children have access to sufficient levels of key nutrients and decent healthcare. Accordingly, providing adequate nutrition and access to healthcare is included under the category sustenance (i.e., conditions needed to sustain life).

Many children suffer from poor nutrition and poor eating habits, resulting in compromises to brain development and health (Black et al., 2015; Rosales et al., 2009). Evidence about the advantages of breastfeeding has become more convincing (Grummer-Strawn et al., 2014; Robinson & Fall, 2012). However, it can be a challenge for working mothers to breastfeed children (Pearce et al., 2012). To prevent potential nutritional problems from infancy onward requires that caregivers watch what children eat, establish good eating routines, and model healthy eating (Palfreyman et al., 2014).

Low household income often leads to inadequate food consumption, sometimes from just having too little to eat and sometimes from poor eating habits. However, relations between household income and nutritional intake are anything but simple (Kant & Graubard, 2012). There is no consistency in how parents respond to food shortage. Factors such as the type of work done by parents and societal values feed into the equation, as do struggles parents may face when dealing with mental illness and substance abuse disorders (Hurley et al., 2015; Janevic et al., 2010; Smith et al., 2016; Zeitlin, 1996). Dietary intake tends to vary as a consequence of where people live as well (Pearson et al., 2009; Rasmussen et al., 2006). Residential areas vary with respect to the general level of social organization present and with respect to the kinds of foods that are available, both of which can have a bearing on the dietary intake of family members (Allcott et al., 2019; Saelens et al., 2018).

As children grow, they are likely to sustain injuries and to confront viruses, bacteria, and other pathogens that can affect their health. Consequently, they need access to good medical care (Regalado & Halfon, 2001). Surveys point to marked differences in the kinds of healthcare that is accessible to families both within and across nations (Delamater et al., 2012; Health and Places Initiative, 2014; Radley & Schoen, 2012). Consequently, parents who live in areas where access to healthcare (basic or more specialized) is limited will likely take different actions to serve children's health needs than will parents with ready access to particular forms of healthcare.

More limited access to medical care may partially account for the fact that rural children receive less preventive healthcare and show higher rates of childhood mortality (Probst et al., 2018). However, the primary causes of child deaths (drowning, motor vehicle accident, firearms, and farm machinery) suggest that other features of rural habitats are major contributors as well (US Department of Health and Human Services, 2017). Unfortunately, there have been relatively few studies comparing the eating patterns and other lifestyle patterns for families living in different geographic areas, with findings being inconsistent across studies (McCormack & Meendering, 2016). Accordingly, observed urban/rural differences in health problems and mortality rates could reflect a diversity of mechanisms: (1) more rural families tend to be poor and (2) some rural families live a great distance from high-quality grocery stores and medical care facilities. It is important to bear in mind that cultural beliefs and connections with social networks can also have a bearing on parental decisions with respect to feeding and use of healthcare pertaining to children (Hajizadeh et al., 2016; Martin et al., 2004).

6.2 Safety

The limited capabilities of children make them especially vulnerable to injury. The leading cause of morbidity and mortality in children beyond age one is accidents, many of which are preventable (Centers for Disease Control, 2015). Thus, it is incumbent upon caregivers to proactively address potential safety issues. An example is the use of car restraints (American Academy of Pediatrics, 2016).

Caregivers need to employ an array of strategies to protect children from injury at home and outside. These include keeping dangerous objects out of reach, restricting a child's access to places and objects that pose injury risk, and carefully supervising children (Ablewhite et al., 2015). As children get older, adults can provide guidance to children about how to avoid dangerous situations and how to get help if needed. Guidance on how to deal with potential hazards is important particularly if the family lives in an area that is dilapidated or high in crime (Bradley, Corwyn, McAdoo et al., 2001; Dercon & Krishnan, 2009).

The precise strategies caregivers need to use to assure child safety depend on the conditions present in and around the residence. Children in rural areas are more likely to die from burns, drowning, and motor vehicle accidents than are their urban counterparts, as the outdoor conditions differ in the two types of habitats (Leonhard et al., 2015; US Department of Health and Human Services, 2015). Part of the difference likely reflects generally lower wealth and education among rural parents and part likely reflects differences in cultural values, the latter leading to different expectations pertaining to monitoring of children's whereabouts (Valentine, 1997). Not surprisingly, low-SES homes, wherever they are located, often have more safety hazards than the homes of well-to-do families (Gielen et al., 2012). As children get older and are allowed to wander (unsupervised) into the neighborhood, injuries are more likely, especially in rundown residential areas (Bradley, Corwyn, McAdoo et al., 2001; Dercon & Krishnam, 2009).

Even though parents are generally inclined to protect their children, not all parents are able to do so in a consistent manner. Parents with mental illness often find it difficult to engage in the kinds of parenting practices needed to support their children (Kohl et al., 2011). As Section 7 on contextual challenges makes clear, anything that increases parental stress can make it more difficult for parents to remain alert in ways that assure child safety (McEwen & Gianaros, 2010). Likewise, when parents abuse alcohol and drugs, they are less likely to engage in the kinds of behaviors necessary to assure child safety (Barnard & McKeganey, 2004; Lipari & Van Horn, 2017). Exposure to toxins is also exceptionally likely for children who live with parents who use and/or manufacture drugs (e.g., methamphetamines: Hayward et al., 2010). The US Department of Health and Human Services (2019) released a report showing that both parental mental illness and parental drug abuse increased the likelihood that children were removed from their homes due to fears for their safety.

6.3 Stimulation

As complex, multisensory creatures, humans benefit from many forms of stimulation (Bransford et al., 2000). Caregiver efforts to stimulate children can take many forms, such as talking to them, reading to them, teaching them specific skills, playing with them, involving them in household activities, outside excursions, and family projects. There is now substantial support for the idea that stimulation from people, objects, and events is important for cognitive, social, and psychomotor development (Baker, 2013; Bradley, Corwyn, Burchinal et al., 2001; Gilkerson et al., 2018). With advances in technology and concomitant changes in the world of work, the advantages of exposure to high-quality stimulation have multiplied. To move from novice learner to expert in any particular area of knowledge or skill requires substantial experience in that area (LeFevre et al., 2010; Manolitsis et al., 2013). Neurocognitive studies show that the quantity and quality of stimulation available to a child influences brain structure and function (Avants et al., 2015; Johnson et al., 2016).

The idea that access to materials promotes skill development has substantial support (LeFevre et al., 2010; Melhuish et al., 2008; Sammons et al., 2015; Tomopoulos et al., 2006). Presenting objects to children contributes to their learning of nouns (i.e., the names of those objects) (McDonough et al., 2011). Access to high levels of materials in the home is associated with sustained interest in particular activities for preschool children (Leibham et al., 2005). New opportunities for meaningful activity are perceived, new types of actions emerge, and new meanings for the actions and objects are constructed. Playing with Lego is a good example. Meaningful play with Lego requires that a child build spatially with large numbers of Lego and to conceive of imaginary structures that represent real objects. That experience fosters better formal operations thinking in the area of mathematics downstream (Wolfgang et al., 2003). In general, when children have access to a large array of potentially stimulating "stuff" (both natural and man-made), it encourages their engagement with the stuff and leads to higher forms of learning. As an example, having communication technology equipment (including internet access) in the home was associated with greater computer and information literacy (Fraillon et al., 2014).

Having toys and objects available in a home increases the likelihood of productive social interactions between household members (Baker, 2013; Tomopolous et al., 2006). When children engage in informal learning activities with a parent (often with books and learning materials), it facilitates their academic performance (Lehrl et al., 2019). Engaging in activities with books, rocks and twigs, iPads, construction toys, and learning materials increases children's interest in those materials and a deeper processing of the experiences related to them (Dearing et al., 2012; Farver et al., 2006).

Exposure to events and experiences outside of the home or school (e.g., FaceTiming with friends and relatives, walks in the forest, trips to the library, ball games, visits to zoos, museums, and neighborhood parks, and excursions to commercial facilities such as supermarkets and shopping malls) also have the potential to promote learning (Bradley & Caldwell, 1984b; Bradley, Corwyn, Burchinal et al., 2001; Bransford et al., 2000). However, it is difficult to precisely determine how any single aspect of the overall conditions of a child's home life is implicated in their development, given the co-occurrence of many forms of stimulation (Bradley, Corwyn, Burchinal et al., 2001). Moreover, households with high levels of resources of one sort often have high levels of resources of other sorts that increase the likelihood of high-quality stimulation for children. For example, when families have a higher income, the adults tend to have high levels of education and strong social networks; and the families often reside in resource-rich communities. High-income parents also tend to have jobs with greater substantive complexity, which leads them to involve their children in more intellectually demanding leisure activities and discourse (Schooler, 1999).

Numerous studies show disparities between the "haves" and "have-nots" with respect to the presence of play and learning materials and the likelihood that parents will read to children, speak to them using complex language, and engage them in other types of encounters that promote learning (Biedinger, 2011; Bradley, Corwyn, McAdoo et al., 2001; Hamadani et al., 2014; Hart & Risley, 1995; Sansour et al., 2011). Parental education, together with income, helps determine whether children will have access to musical instruments, art supplies, and sports equipment (Bradley, Corwyn, Burchinal et al., 2001; Yeung et al., 2002). Income is a major factor in determining whether children will participate in sports, do volunteer work, take music, art, or dance lessons, and participate in organizations like the Scouts (Pew Research Center, 2015). Families with limited income are also more likely to live in crowded conditions, which can increase stress for parents and reduce the likelihood they provide children with high-quality stimulation (Cabrera et al., 2011; Evans et al., 1999). Poor families also tend to have more children, with research suggesting that having more children leads to lower levels of stimulation (Koury & Vortruba-Drzal, 2014). As the penetration of computer technologies into everyday life has deepened, there are particular worries about income disparities in computer and internet access for children, which may limit children's exposure to key educational and social resources (Katz et al., 2017; Rideout & Katz, 2016).

When parents have mental illness or problems with addiction, they are less likely to engage their children in enriching activities (Barnard & McKeganey, 2004; Kiernan & Huerta, 2008; Oyserman et al., 2000). Parents with mental illness or addiction problems more often parent alone and have fewer social and economic resources to call upon in caring for their children (Biedinger, 2011; Kiernan & Huerta, 2008; Koury & Vortruba-Drzal, 2014; Noll et al., 1992; Rubio-Codina et al., 2016; Sansour et al., 2011).

Having access to resources (social and material) at the household, neighborhood, and community level helps determine what parents do to provide stimulation for children. Thus, not having access to key resources, like electricity and the Internet (a particularly serious problem in rural areas of developing countries), can be quite limiting for parents who wish to offer their children diverse types of stimulation (Bradley & Putnick, 2012; Hollingsworth et al., 2011; Ritchie & Roser, 2019a).

Parents in poor countries are less wont to spend time in imaginative play with children or guiding their skill development in ways that connect to academic learning. By contrast, when families reside in somewhat larger and more well-to -do communities, it enables parents to provide other types of stimulating experiences as well – most specifically, whether they provide lessons to support artistic and athletic interests. Critical in this regard is living in reasonably close proximity to facilities and instructors who provide lessons also plays a role in whether a child is given private lessons (Child Trends, 2015; Corrigall & Schellenberg, 2015). In general, it can be difficult for both children and adults to get advanced training in the arts and technology in rural areas (Association of Science-Technology Centers, 2014; Donovan & Brown, 2017; Woodberry, 2017). Somewhat by contrast, children's opportunities for outdoor play have declined over the past half-century, due to the expansion of technology and urbanization, leading concerns that it will reduce opportunities for boisterous play and engagement with natural elements (Maynard & Waters, 2007). Research shows that living near parks and recreational facilities increases the likelihood that children will engage in activities that increase psychomotor skills, including joint activity with parents (Eime et al., 2015). Indeed, studies have shown that communication with parents outdoors tends to be of a higher quality than communication with parents indoors (Cameron-Faulkner et al., 2018). Not surprisingly, living in densely populated, inner-city neighborhoods, particularly with high concentrations of poor families can discourage outdoor activities as parents tend to be overprotective due to worries about safety hazards in the nearby environment (Bartlett, 1999; Bento & Dias, 2017).

Stimulation, in its various forms, has the potential to directly engage intrinsic motives such as curiosity/exploration and mastery. As such, it connects to capacities for self-regulation and self-management (Zimmerman, 2000). In a stimulus-rich environment, there is a much greater likelihood that a child's activity will become goal-directed and productive. The more open-ended an object (or activity) with which a child engages, the more likely its effects will be multiple and wide-ranging, partly owing to the greater likelihood that it will engage children's intrinsic motivations and promote feed-forward loops among areas of competence (Cunha & Heckman, 2007). By contrast, stimulus-poor environments can lead to dysfunctions in self-regulation and even to depression and mood disorders.

Although there is evidence linking access to learning materials and enriching activities with motivation, achievement, and adaptive behavior, such observed relations may not reflect simple causal connections (Senechal & LeFevre, 2002). When settings contain a diverse array of toys, learning materials, and objects, this increases the likelihood of productive interactions between children and adults (Tomopolous et al., 2006). Children who have a higher level of access to growth-enhancing materials and activities at home are also more likely to have access to other social and physical resources that promote skill development as well (Bradley, Corwyn, McAdoo et al., 2001; Greenberg et al., 1999; Yildiz et al., 2018).

6.4 Socioemotional Support

In higher-order species such as humans, becoming socially competent can be challenging given the complexities of everyday life and the varied roles played by others in one's environment (Grusec & Davidov, 2010; Lewis, 2000). For similar reasons, it can be difficult for humans to maintain good emotional health. The biological underpinnings of social and emotional behavior in humans are quite complex (Frith & Frith, 2001; Harmon-Jones et al., 2010; Soto-Icaza et al., 2015). Consequently, it is not surprising that young children often struggle when trying to understand how they should behave and how to deal with their own emotional responses. Young children are often hard-pressed to regulate their behavior when internal or external conditions are challenging (Bronson, 2000). To cope with anxieties and feelings of insecurity, children need vigilant, responsive attention from parents and other caregivers, attention that engenders a sense of trust and confidence (Bowlby, 1969; Bretherton &

Waters, 1985). There is evidence that human infants need caregiver proximity and touch to avoid feeling distressed (Norholt, 2020). Parental responsiveness is instrumental in helping children learn how to engage in productive reciprocal exchanges, a skill that is critical to long-term success in a world that involves ongoing interactions with others (Criss et al., 2003; Grusec & Davidov, 2010). If children receive responsive support from caregivers and live in an environment that affords them protection from forces that would undermine adaptive functioning, they tend to move toward social competence and emotional health (Egger & Angold, 2006). By contrast, when caregivers are unresponsive to children or treat them harshly, it undermines the development of self-regulation and mastery motivation (Blair & Raver, 2012).

According to parental acceptance–rejection theory, parental warmth helps support positive adjustment, good health, and competence in children (Rohner et al., 2005). Children benefit from positive affirmation of worth, as this initiates a process of self-affirmation and makes a child both more resilient against stressors and more likely to productively engage with people and tasks (Cohen & Sherman, 2014). To fully appreciate the connection between caregiver socioemotional support and child well-being, it is important to understand that adults from different cultures are likely to express affection, affirm worth, or act in a responsive way toward their children using different forms (Agrawal & Gulati, 2005; Bornstein et al., 2015; Chao & Kanatsu, 2008; Keller et al., 2004; Richman et al., 1988; Whiting & Edwards, 1988). Even so, in almost all societies, ignoring or shaming a young child conveys a lack of interest or worthiness; and it has negative impacts on children's adaptive behavior (Manly et al., 2013).

There is an expectation in most societies that individuals can control their behavior, a skill that is not easy for young children (Bronson, 2000). To facilitate the development of behavioral control, parents must engage in productive discipline strategies. Although issues surrounding the use of corporal punishment remain controversial, there is ample evidence that harsh and inconsistent punishment has negative consequences for children's adaptive behavior (Burlaka et al., 2017; Gershoff, 2013). By contrast, discipline styles that include more use of reasoning, problem-solving, and consistent limit-setting are associated with more optimal outcomes (Hart et al., 1992; Larzelere, 2000). These general associations notwithstanding, there are sociocultural differences in the use and consequences of more restrictive and controlling forms of discipline (Whaley, 2000).

As children develop, it becomes increasingly important that caregivers prepare them for life outside the family and immediate home context; that is, to inculcate what is sometimes called emotional intelligence (Petrides et al., 2006).

Caregivers can facilitate emotional intelligence by providing encouragement and by offering guidance on how to appraise situations and act thoughtfully during social interactions (Pettit et al., 1988).

Contextual factors help determine the likelihood that caregivers will enact particular forms of socioemotional support (Bornstein, 2015). The presence of siblings is an interesting example. Not surprisingly, conflict between siblings leads to harsher, more restrictive parenting (Feinberg et al., 2012). Research also shows that absorption in using the phone can have a negative impact on parenting. Not only can the stresses connected with using a phone while trying to manage a child lead to lower parental responsiveness toward children, but it sometimes leads to greater hostility as well (McDaniel, 2019).

When stressors are present in the family or broader social context, it decreases the likelihood parents will manifest positive social behaviors toward children and it increases the likelihood they will manifest negative ones (Conger et al. 2010; Mistry et al., 2008). Stress is particularly common in low-SES households; and it can lead to less nurturant, more hostile interactions between parents and children (Blair & Raver, 2012; Bradley, Corwyn, Burchinal et al., 2001; Gunning et al., 2004; Kiernan & Huerta, 2008). Low-income families often live in crowded residences, a condition that can increase tensions (see Section 7.1.3). In general, crowding reduces the likelihood that parents will be warm and responsive to children (Bradley & Caldwell, 1984b; Evans et al., 2010; Thornock et al., 2019). Chaos is more common in low-SES households too, with research showing that confusion in the house decreases maternal responsiveness (Corapci & Wachs, 2002). Household chaos also increases the likelihood that parents will display negative behavior toward children and can lead to inconsistent and ineffective disciplinary practices (Coldwell et al., 2006; Dumas et al., 2005).

Living in a rundown neighborhood sometimes reduces parental expressions of warmth and increases punitiveness; albeit the findings are mixed (Gonzales et al., 2011; Vieno et al., 2010). The evidence pertaining to neighborhood disadvantage, while limited, suggests that the influence is greater for low-income families and immigrant families with low levels of acculturation (Barnett et al., 2012; Cueller et al., 2015; Kohen et al., 2008). The impacts seem more likely if families have been exposed to community violence (Aisenberg & Ell, 2005). In such situations, children and parents are likely to become more anxious, sometimes feeding off each other's insecurities. Some of the negative impact of living in a low-income urban area also seems partially offset if there are nearby green spaces, but the positive impacts seem mostly for women (Roe et al., 2013).

MacKinnon and colleagues (1982) and Bradley and Caldwell (1984b) found that single-parent households scored lower in acceptance and responsiveness on the HOME Inventory. In general, it appears that social support can partially mitigate the negative impact of adverse circumstances on parenting (Ceballo & McLoyd, 2002; McConnell et al., 2011; Taylor et al., 2015). Spousal support, in particular, is associated with greater involvement and more nurturant care in both mothers (Cummings & Davies, 2002; Olsen et al., 1999) and fathers (Bonney et al., 1999; NICHD Early Child Care Research Network, 2000). By contrast, Belsky and colleagues (1997) found that unsupportive co-parenting was associated with less responsive parenting for both mothers and fathers. Interparental conflict increases the likelihood that parents will act in harsh and punitive ways toward children, what is called a "spillover" effect (Krishnakumar & Buehler, 2000). Intimate partner violence also increases the likelihood that mothers will be neglectful (Banyard et al., 2003; Lannert et al., 2014). Unfortunately, the construct of social support is a bit "fuzzy" in what it represents. It has not been conceived or measured in a consistent way in studies of human behavior (Geens & Vandenbroeck, 2012).

A caregiver's personal history and personality influence how much socio-emotional support a caregiver is likely to provide a child. Children who live with parents who have serious mental health and addiction problems tend to experience more household chaos, thus increasing their anxiety and often reducing their opportunities for enriching stimulation as well as positive communication with parents and others (Mattejat & Remschmidt, 2008). Mental illness also decreases the likelihood that parents will be emotionally responsive to their children (Howard et al., 2001; Kiernan & Huerta, 2008; Lovejoy et al., 2000; Oyserman et al., 2000; Wilson & Durbin, 2010).

At present, there is limited information on how often parents offer most types of socioemotional support to children. Likewise, not much is known regarding how various aspects of the social and physical environment change the rate at which parents provide supportive actions and conditions for their children. Longitudinal studies that consider multiple types of socioemotional support and that look at multiple potential moderators of their use and impact would, therefore, be quite helpful.

6.5 Surveillance

Almost every parent can recount those moments when a preschooler vanished from view in a department store and when a school-age child jumped out of the car to run into McDonald's. The popular press is also full of stories about the actions of "latch key" children. All of these accounts make clear the value of keeping tabs on children. To effectively manage children's lives, caregivers must keep track of their activities and whereabouts (i.e., surveillance). Injuries are more common when parents fail to adequately supervise young children (Morrongiello et al., 2011).

Adequate supervision of children requires knowing not just where a child is but the conditions present in whatever setting the child occupies. Conditions vary enormously across settings and even within the same setting (Belanger & Coolen, 2014). Much tighter monitoring is needed when a toddler is in a bathtub than when the same toddler is watching TV (Simon et al., 2003). Each setting, whether inside the home, nearby the residence, or in locations where families go for business or pleasure, imposes its own particular pressures on parents in terms of maintaining visual or physical contact with a child. Greater vigilance is generally required in malls and near busy streets than in a church or an upscale neighborhood playground. How best to monitor depends on a child's proclivities, competence, and personal history (Morrongiello et al., 2008; Waylen & McKenna, 2009; Wells et al., 2012).

When families live in dangerous or dilapidated neighborhoods, there is a tendency for parents to monitor children more closely and be more restrictive (Jones et al., 2005; O'Neil et al., 2001; Stace & Roker, 2005). However, there is no evidence for strong neighborhood effects (Cueller et al., 2015).

The pervasiveness of media devices in today's world makes it more difficult for parents to effectively monitor children's activities. Parents' own use of smartphones and other media sometimes reduces careful monitoring of their children (Jago et al., 2012). Most parents report checking the websites their children have visited and their social media profiles, and they report looking through phone call records (Pew Research Center, 2016) – albeit such forms of monitoring largely apply to older children. Even so, many parents are somewhat ambivalent as regards how much to monitor and control children's use of media (Nikken & Schols, 2015; Pew Research Center, 2016). For this reason, the American Academy of Pediatrics has constructed a Family Media Use Plan they hope will reduce the amount of time spent by both adults and children using media (Chassiakos et al., 2016).

Providing optimal surveillance of children can be difficult in some situations. A good example is when a child is at home alone (Belle, 1999). More well-to-do parents sometimes install video equipment to help with the process; and even less well-to-do parents sometimes use phone calls or texting to help keep track on child behavior (Hartwell-Rocker, 2018). In households where there is only one parent, research points to a reduction in monitoring and a higher risk of injury (Chao & Kanatsu, 2008; Rivara & Mueller, 1987). By contrast, in households where there are other kith and kin to help with daily tasks, the burden of monitoring can be distributed across the networks of adults and older children (Dunifon & Bairacharya, 2012). However, monitoring by older siblings is not always optimal and can lead to injuries in young children (Morrongiello et al., 2007; Ruiz-Casares et al., 2018).

Parental perceptions about the level of surveillance their children needs reflect the parent's assessment of the controllability of the hazards present in specific settings; and it reflects the caregiver's overall supervisory style (Ablewhite et al, 2015; Stace & Roker, 2005). Unfortunately, parents often overestimate children's capacity to understand the dangers present in situations or to control their proclivities to engage with the environment (Karstad et al., 2014). Perhaps nothing more accurately conveys parental misunderstanding of children's capacities than drowning or near-drowning episodes, with lapses in adult monitoring and supervision identified as the most common factor connected to these incidences (Brenner & the Committee on Injury, Violence, and Poison Prevention, 2003).

Although most research on parental surveillance pertains to their efforts to reduce harm, parents must also monitor the extent to which children engage in activities that promote key life skills. A good example is checking to see if the child is doing homework and if conditions surrounding the child are supportive of the child's engagement in homework (Hoover-Dempsey et al., 2001). The effectiveness of these monitoring strategies is not yet clear, however. Research suggests that parental monitoring and supervision of children's academic activities is likely to be more productive if accompanied by parental warmth, good communication, and behaviors that promote child autonomy (Dettmers et al., 2019). To fully understand the role played by parental surveillance in children's lives, it will be necessary to substantially expand the focus of studies in the area to include the forms of surveillance parents use to promote various skills as well as to protect children from harm; and to look at the interplay of surveillance and other caregiving behaviors (e.g., warmth, structure, behavioral control).

6.6 Structure

Optimal development requires careful arrangement of social and physical inputs so that it is easy for a child to uptake positive inputs and cope with challenges. When conditions at home are orderly and transparent, it is easier for family members to act productively. As the preceding sections make clear, children need much from their environments to do well; and parents have multiple tasks to perform to promote child well-being. Accordingly, parents must organize how and when various inputs get to the child and organize time, space, objects, and events that occur in settings so that there is a "fit" between a child's needs and what the setting affords (Spagnola & Fiese, 2007; Walsh et al., 2000).

When daily life has structure and consistency, children are more likely to display adaptive behavior; whereas, household chaos can lead to poor overall health (Dush et al., 2013). The need for fit between daily conditions and child skills is especially consequential for children whose temperaments make them highly reactive to environmental conditions (Kagan, 2003). In effect, both children and parents can function more productively when the conditions are orderly and transparent.

When thinking about fit between what a child needs and what the environment affords, consider what might seem a mundane task – feeding a child. It is not enough that the parent provides sufficient nourishment. Poor timing and pacing of feeding may contribute to failure to thrive (Drotar, 1985) or childhood obesity (Anderson & Whitaker, 2010). Likewise, children are more likely to benefit from learning opportunities when someone organizes a child's encounters with objects and ideas in ways that are easier for the child to assimilate, what learning professionals call scaffolding (Hammond et al., 2012). Parental scaffolding of children's early language experiences (i.e., providing a predictable referential and social context for communication) contributes to language acquisition (Bruner, 1983). Likewise, parents can foster math competence by offering feedback and strategies during games that require some type of numeric reasoning (Bjorklund et al., 2004); and reading competence is improved when adults engage a child in an ongoing dialog about what is going on in pictures presented on each page of a book rather than just reading the story to the child (Brannon & Daukas, 2014). There is a growing literature on how adults can organize (or "scaffold") children's learning so that a child's engagement in a learning activity is more productive (Blewitt et al., 2009; Pea, 2004). However, careful scaffolding of children's learning can be more challenging for single parents and less educated parents (Anderson & Whitaker, 2010; Lowe et al., 2013; Stright et al., 2009).

Some young children find it difficult to transition from one activity to another, one caregiver to another, or one place to another. Parents can provide orderly assistance for such transitions by doing things like having consistent patterns of drop-off and pick-up for children who go to childcare., a task that is harder when a child has multiple forms of nonparental care (Morrissey, 2009). Likewise, the transition to formal school can be difficult for some children. Preparing a child for going to school and having regular school day routines can assist with the process of transition (Sandstrom & Huerta, 2013).

Life is full of changes, many of which require adjustment in family routines or routines for children. Consider two commonplace changes: seasonal changes and changes in daily schedules from weekdays to weekends. Parents often arrange for children to be more physically active during weekends and over the summer (Atkin et al., 2016). However, even commonplace changes in family life (moving to a new neighborhood, birth of a sibling, military deployment, change of jobs, joining a sport team) can sometimes lead to major shifts in family routines or physical arrangements within the household (Martin et al., 2012; Mayberry et al., 2014; Roche & Ghazarian, 2012). Given children's limited planning skills, parental efforts to provide organization can loom large in such times of change. During times of significant change, children fare better when parents foster a continuing sense of family cohesion and a sense that there is manageability in life (Bradley et al., 1994; Zolkoski & Bullock, 2012). Doing so can be difficult when families experience trauma, since the parents themselves may be dislocated and emotionally overwhelmed (Banyard et al., 2003; Gerwitz et al., 2008).

In general, when families experience stressful life events, it can lead to disorder at home. Parental inability to offset the disorder connected to stressful life events can lead to emotional distress and poor achievement for children (Chen et al., 2010; Muniz et al., 2014). Experiencing negative life events, and the chaos they sometimes bring, is often part of a larger set of factors, such as being poor or living in a crowded home, that make the implementation of positive routines and household organization difficult (Evans & Wachs, 2010; McLoyd et al., 2008).

Involvement with media devices is changing much about family dynamics and how parents manage common daily activities (Villegas, 2013). Most critically, perhaps, they are changing the structure of interpersonal interactions and how family members communicate (Misra et al., 2014; Przybylski & Weinstein, 2012). The emergence of new forms of media and electronic devices has motivated parents of young children to actively mediate children's engagement with the devices, to enhance enjoyment and learning (Nikken & Schols, 2015).

Where families live can also have a bearing on what parents are likely to do to structure a child's daily life. Bornstein (2015) made the case that parental beliefs (including those about their surroundings) help determine the kind of childrearing practices a parent is likely to employ. In dilapidated neighborhoods, parents tend to reduce the child's exploration of the nearby environment (McDonnell, 2007). The quality and resources available in the neighborhood and community affect the kinds of regulatory strategies parents use and children's social competence (O'Neil et al., 2001). Where a family resides and the cultural beliefs present in that location can be instrumental in shaping how a parent organizes time, objects, and actions connected with childrearing.

Parents with substance abuse problems tend to be inconsistent in maintaining productive, orderly patterns of household activities (Lander et al., 2013; Romanowicz et al., 2019; Smith et al., 2016). Poor household organization is also more likely if a parent is mentally ill, has conflicts with other adults in the household, or experiences other forms of stress (Solis et al., 2012). Indeed, parental substance abuse is often a marker for a host of negative risks (e.g., various forms of instability) that increase the likelihood of disorderly parenting and poor adjustment for children (Leonard & Eiden, 2007).

Mental illness often co-occurs with substance abuse (Substance Abuse & Mental Health Services Administration, 2019); and adults with mental illness often struggle to maintain order in their lives (Solis et al., 2012). Assessments of parents with mental illness suggest a limited capacity to engage in productive parenting in a consistent manner (Boursnell, 2014; Shenoy et al., 2019; Simpson-Adkins & Daiches, 2018). Not surprisingly, parents with mental illness find it difficult to obtain and maintain high-level employment, which can complicate their ability to maintain household order (Hoffman et al., 2006; Luciano et al., 2014; National Research Council & Institute of Medicine, 2009).

Providing structure in children's lives takes many forms; thus, it is not surprising that very little is known about the implications of most forms of parental structure or even how often parents provide such forms. As has been discussed in this and prior sections, almost every type of input to children seems to have a more positive effect if the input itself is consistently provided and if the input occurs in a generally orderly environment; albeit research provides limited detail on the interplay of most specific forms of structure and most specific forms of other types of caregiving.

6.7 Social Integration

For children to succeed, they must become connected to the social fabric of society. It is through connections with other members of society and societal institutions (e.g., extended family, adults in the community, work associates, community organizations and agencies) that children receive many of the supports and opportunities they need to live productively (Weisner, 2002). Consequently, parents need to act in ways that secure such connections.

Having positive connections with social networks and community groups can be especially useful for families living in adverse circumstances (Horvat et al., 2003). Unfortunately, poor, single-parent mothers tend to have smaller social networks, making it more difficult to connect their children with supportive adults (Barajas, 2011). Likewise, parents who abuse substances or who have mental illness are less likely to have a strong social network or good connections with key social agencies (Howard et al., 2001: National Research Council & Institute of Medicine, 2009; Semple et al., 2001).

For most parents, the starting point for building a child's social connections is with extended family and close friends. It entails setting up circumstances where a child spends time with adults and other children in these intimate social networks, thereby promoting connections (Raising Children Network, 2020). A savvy parent sets up activities that are enjoyable for both child and others and helps structure activities so they are easy for the child to manage. The next step in fostering good social connections involves having the child spend time with people outside the immediate family (in childcare, at church, at a neighborhood park). These encounters increase the likelihood a child will make connections with others; and they can promote the development of autonomy and self-identity (Grusec, 2011).

If parents have a large friendship network, it is easier for them to put their children in contact with playmates (Guralnick et al., 2009; Iaupuni et al., 2005). Parents can also connect young children to peers and adults by enrolling them in childcare and preschools. Social networks provide potentially useful information about community agencies and programs that provide platforms for children's social integration into society as well as provide children opportunities for learning and enjoyment (Curry et al., 2016). As children age, parental involvement with school personnel and school activities provides their children with additional opportunities to connect with key members of the community (Pianta & Walsh, 1996).

In most communities, there are groups and institutions that afford parents opportunities to increase their own social ties as well as promote social connections for their children, including churches, libraries, and childcare providers (Assari, 2013; Hancock et al., 2015; Ostrosky & Meadan, 2010; Pew Research Center, 2013). Critical throughout childhood is that caregivers connect children to other adults whom they can trust, for it is trusted relationships with adults that help determine how children spend their time and their ongoing well-being (Meltzer et al., 2018).

Poverty at the household, neighborhood, and country levels generally make it difficult for parents to foster or maintain good social connections (De Silva & Harpham, 2007; Horvat et al., 2003; Runyan et al. 1998; Stack & Meredith, 2018). The multiple challenges often associated with low financial and material resources can lead to parental withdrawal both from their children and from others who might assist their children (Conger et al., 2010; Evans & Kim, 2013). In addition, low-SES parents are likely to have employment situations that make it more difficult to maintain good family routines and robust social connections (Sheely, 2010). By contrast, high-SES parents are better able not only to form connections with others but also to work with others toward a common purpose (Horvat et al., 2003). Higher-SES parents tend to have greater social capital as a function of the jobs they have and the neighborhoods in which they live. This enables their children to go to schools and form connections with peer groups and adults that enhance their life's prospects, what is sometimes referred to as social capital bridging (Crosnoe & Muller, 2014; Parcel & Bixby, 2016).

Where families live has a bearing on the actions they are likely to take to foster social connections for their children. In poor countries and neighborhoods, there tends to be less social cohesion, which often translates to less community involvement with children and fewer opportunities for parents to form social ties that increase social integration for children (Cueller et al., 2015; Minh et al., 2017). Even in places where families historically lived in cohesive communities, poverty, migration, and internal strife have reduced the levels of social cohesion now present (United Nations Economic Commission for Africa, 2016). In neighborhoods with high social cohesion, there are more opportunities for parents to form social ties with community members in ways that bring social capital to their children.

It is not just the neighborhood or the quality of residences present that helps determine how likely it is that parents will make useful social connections. Physical attributes matter as well. In some communities, streets are easier to traverse and more pleasant to walk down. Some are more "child-friendly," in that they present fewer threats to children and may even motivate child play and productive behavior (Islam et al., 2016). In child-friendly areas, both parent and child are likely to engage with others. Living in a rural area sometimes has advantages for socially integrating children into society (e.g., rural residents are more likely to know others in the community). However, rural areas typically do not contain settings that increase the likelihood of engaging others (day-care centers, libraries, museums, facilities for lessons) (Henly & Adams, 2018; Henning-Smith & Kozhimannil, 2016; Provasnik et al., 2007; Swan et al., 2013).

6.8 Less Is More

Not everything parents do on behalf of their children can be neatly subsumed under the seven broad parenting tasks described in this section. Moreover, a single act on the part of a parent could fulfill more than a single goal for a child. That said, the vast literature on parenting indicates that when parents accomplish these seven tasks in a sustained and consistent manner it bodes well for children – perhaps, particularly when the children have biological or environmental risks (Bradley et al., 1994). However, exposure to risks, such as poverty, household chaos, and negative life events tends to undermine parental efforts to productively engage in all seven parenting tasks (Bradley, 2017).

Research on how parenting affects child well-being (and how the environment more generally affects child well-being) has often been driven by concerns that children were not getting enough of some sort of "good thing." The idea that more is always better came under greater scrutiny (Bornstein & Manian, 2013). For example, studies aimed at better understanding how caregiver contingent responsiveness connects to infant attachment security have shown that over-contingency might actually work against building secure attachment and self-reliance (Jaffee et al., 2001; van den Boom, 1994). Bornstein and Manian (2013) found a curvilinear relation between maternal contingent behavior in the moment and overall sensitivity – positive up to a point and then increasingly negative.

There is now greater attention to issues such as overstimulation (such as was addressed in a limited manner in Section 5.1 on media and will be addressed in Sections 7.1.2 and 7.1.3 dealing with noise and crowding respectively). Studies in humans and animals have shown that social and sensory overstimulation can lead to deficits in cognitive performance and to autistic-like behaviors (Christakis et al., 2012; Favre et al, 2015). Indeed, it appears that humans are wired so that our brains do not become overwhelmed when trying to deal with too much information at one time (Tabor et al., 2018).

As stated in Section 6.6 dealing with structure, optimal development entails finding a good fit between children's needs and proclivities and what the environment affords. In recognition of the fact that high levels of regulation and organization can sometimes work against meeting human needs, research has increased on the potential negative consequences of overscheduling children's lessons and activities (Barker et al., 2014; Mahoney et al., 2006). Research does not yet make clear how much scheduling is too much or how many activities are too many (Wedge, 2014). However, research indicates that overcontrolling early in a child's life can reduce the development of self-regulatory skills, with longer-term impacts on adjustment (Perry et al., 2018). In general, more research is needed on how inputs from parents above a moderate level contribute to children's development, with the idea that there might be either thresholds beyond which more is not better or even points beyond which more is counterproductive.

7 Contextual Challenges

This section will focus on aspects of context that often present challenges to both caregivers and children – albeit these aspects may also afford greater opportunities as well. The focus will be on challenges that are social, physical, and organizational in nature.

7.1 Instability

Positive adaptation in children requires predictability and controllability in the settings where they spend time (Carver & Conner-Smith, 2010). Both children and caregivers tend to struggle when life is infused by unstable conditions, like moves, family dissolution, and major interruptions in household conditions (Sandstrom & Huerta, 2013).

7.1.1 Chaos

When households are orderly and families have good routines, children tend to be more socially and emotionally ready to engage in everyday activities, including schoolwork (Muniz et al., 2014). By contrast, household chaos tends to interfere with social, emotional, and cognitive functioning (Dumas et al., 2005; Evans et al., 2005; Petrill et al., 2004; Vernon-Feagans et al., 2012). Dush and colleagues (2013) found that crowded, noisy, and cluttered household conditions contributed to poor health in preschoolers, even controlling for key confounders, such as marital status, maternal education, ethnicity, maternal and paternal age, child health status, and household income. Relations between household chaos and less optimal child functioning seem to occur because chaos produces stress in children and because it degrades the care provided to children (Coldwell et al. 2006; Dumas et al., 2005; Jaffee et al., 2012).

7.1.2 Noise

Constant – even intermittent – exposure to excessive levels of noise is distracting and contributes to stress and a sense of learned helplessness (Evans, 2006). Some of the noise children experience at home emanates from within (e.g., loud music or TV), but more often noise penetrates into the interior as a consequence of the home's location near major highways, railways, airports, or industrial sites. For example, living near a major airport has negative impacts on long-term memory and reading achievement in school-age children (Hygge et al., 2002; Stansfeld & Clark, 2015). Exposure to noise can reduce sleep quality for children (Ohrstrom et al., 2006; Stansfeld & Clark, 2015). Ongoing exposure to noise can also contribute to elevated blood pressure and neuroendocrine stress hormones in both children and adults (Babisch et al., 2009; Evans et al., 1998; Regecova & Kellcrova, 1995).

Although the broad impact of excessive noise exposure seems reasonably clear, more research is needed to precisely determine the role noise plays as part of the overall conditions present in children's lives (Casey et al., 2017). Many children exposed to high levels of noise are also exposed to a variety of other risk factors; thus, it can be difficult to pinpoint the exact role played by noise exposure in poor development (Bradley, 2017; Evans et al., 2013). Unfortunately, most research on noise exposure has not been done with a consideration of cumulative risk exposure (Evans et al., 2013).

7.1.3 Crowding

The negative consequences of crowding have long been of concern for those interested in the health and adaptive functioning of children (Evans, 2006). So much so that the World Health Organization (WHO) identified overcrowding at both the individual residence and the neighborhood level as a major source of health problems, especially health problems connected with disease transmission. However, findings implicating crowding in health problems are inconsistent; and many studies lack adequate controls over confounders (Clair, 2019).

Because academic success is becoming increasingly important in a world where technologies pervade the workplace, there is concern about the negative impact of household crowding on cognitive processing and school performance (Goux & Maurin, 2003; Lien et al., 2008). Reading, working on class assignments, and other types of learning can be difficult in places where a child cannot avoid noise and other distractions due to insufficient space (Cox, 2018). That said, findings pertaining to crowding and academic performance are inconsistent, with some evidence indicating that relations vary by age (Evans, 2006; Solari & Mare, 2012).

A major concern of policy makers is how living in crowded homes and densely populated residential neighborhoods can impact children's mental health and may increase maladaptive behavior (Gruebner et al., 2017). Studies involving families from diverse geographic areas demonstrate that crowded conditions are associated with physiological stress and adjustment problems in children (Evans, 2006; Hunt, 1990). Solari and Mare (2012), using data from the Los Angeles Family and Neighborhood Survey (LA FANS) and the Panel Study of Income Dynamics, observed a positive relation between household crowding and maladaptive behavior in children. Their conclusion was that living in a confined space increases the likelihood of personal stress and poor treatment by others in the household.

7.1.4 Migration

A number of factors can contribute to instability in family life, migration being a clear example (Crespi, 2014; International Organization of Migration, 2014). How disruptive migration is on family life depends on what drove families to leave their place of origin (Bornstein, 2017). It tends to be easier if the move is voluntary (e.g., hopes of a better job opportunity) versus involuntary (e.g., war, forced migration, or natural disaster) (Lai & Maclean, 2011). In cases where involuntary migration entails family separation, it can be traumatic for children (Miller et al., 2018; Suarez-Orozco & Suarez-Orozco, 2001). That said, the level of stress produced by migration depends on a number of factors, including the capacity of migrants to accommodate to the ways of living in the country of destination (Van Acker & Vanbeselaere, 2012).

Migration can change a parent's sense of identity, including exactly how best to perform the role of parent. According to Watters (2008), migrant parents may find themselves in kind of a "push/pull" dilemma. The parents feel a pull from the country of origin to maintain certain routines and approaches to parenting, while at the same time feeling a push to implement new approaches that seem better suited to the country of destination. The push/pull dilemma can be all the more paramount in the case of refugees. For migrants who settle into enclaves composed of former residents of their countries of origin, it may be easier to adjust due to shared expectations (Kosic et al., 2008). Even so, the struggle to establish new routines and strategies for parenting can be difficult due to the unfamiliarity of the new setting; and there are likely to be more disruptions during the settling-in process as well.

7.1.5 Residential Moves

When families move, family life is likely to undergo some level of disruption, with evidence suggesting that the impact on children generally depends on circumstances connected with the move (Beck et al., 2016; Murphey et al., 2012). Negative impacts are more likely in the case of forced evictions (Desmond & Kimbro, 2016). Part of the challenge in determining how much residential mobility factors into parenting and child development derives from the fact that some people move to a location with better overall conditions, whereas others move to a place with poorer overall conditions. When children move from a low-poverty neighborhood to a high-poverty neighborhood, it can impair their self-regulatory competence; whereas the opposite is more likely when children move from high-poverty to low-poverty neighborhoods (Roy et al., 2014). Another challenge in interpreting findings pertaining to residential mobility is that moves often co-occur with key risk factors (single-parent status, family dissolution, parental substance abuse, parental mental illness); and moving can sometimes result in disruptions in access to healthcare, childcare, and school (Jelleyman & Spencer, 2008).

7.1.6 Family Dissolution/Structural Change

When families go through separation or divorce, everyday routines are often disrupted, which can increase stress in both children and parents (Ryan & Claessens, 2013; Sandstrom & Huerta, 2013). When parents separate, children sometimes change residences, childcare arrangements, and the schools they attend (Crosnoe et al., 2014). In such cases, family dissolution can lead to loss of friends and familiar places to play or engage in enriching activities (Sparks, 2016). Divorce often results in lower household income and changes in job schedules (Briggs et al., 2019). It can also lead to adjustment problems, especially if the divorce results in substantial reductions in the resources available to families and the kind of caregiving children receive from biological and stepparents (Lansford, 2009; Lee & McLanahan, 2015; Ryan & Claessens, 2013; Wallerstein & Lewis, 2007). Lower parental sensitivity and reduced quality of the home environment are commonplace after divorce (Cavanagh & Huston, 2006).

There is substantial variability in how both children and adults respond to particular forms of instability. As Bornstein (2017) makes clear, the impacts on children can vary according to the characteristics of a child and the broader contextual conditions present. For example, in the case of family dissolution, the impact on children often depends on the quality of co-parenting that follows separation of household members (Lamela & Figueriredo, 2016). Impacts can also vary in terms of the developmental system affected and the duration of effect (i.e., for one child, a disruptive event may reduce academic achievement over a limited period of time; for a second child, it may increase anxiety for years – *multifinality*).

7.2 Interparental Conflict

Very little is as challenging to child well-being as conflict between parents (Wathen & MacMillan, 2013; Whiteside-Mansell et al., 2009). Children, especially young children, tend to have elevated emotional responses when they witness conflict between caregivers. Continuous exposure to conflict can lead to emotional insecurity and chronic stress, particularly if parents do not resolve conflicts in a constructive way (Cummings & Davies, 2002; Horn et al., 2017; Koolick et al., 2016). Children are likely to cope better when parents help them understand and manage their emotions (Dunn & Brown, 1994). Unfortunately, family conflict often leads to disruptions in the family structure and to other forms of instability that threaten children's well-being (e.g., residential moves, changes in childcare or school, reduced involvement with extended family).

7.3 Poor Housing Conditions

Homes without adequate physical facilities increase the likelihood of injuries, illness, and maladaptive behavior (Evans, 2006; Mock et al., 1993; Nriagu et al., 2012; Suglia et al., 2010). Inferior housing conditions can also decrease the quality of caregiving for children, sometimes as a consequence of parental illness or depression (McCracken et al., 2007; Wells & Harris, 2007). Historically, assessments of housing quality have focused on (1) structural materials used to compose the roof, walls, and floors; (2) interior facilities for water, cooking, bathing, and sanitation; and (3) facilities and amenities in the surrounding neighborhood (Fiadzo, 2004; Morenikeji et al., 2017; Yongsi et al., 2007). Studies have consistently shown that families in LMICs (see Section 7.5) often live in homes that have inferior conditions, with concomitant negative impacts on child and adult health (Awasthi et al., 1996; Ezeh et al., 2014; Fuentes et al., 2006; WHO, 2019). A study done in three US cities found that living in poor-quality housing was related to lower socioemotional and cognitive functioning in children of all ages (Coley et al., 2013). The connection between poor housing quality and poor child well-being was mediated by parenting distress and less useful family routines.

7.4 Dilapidated and Dangerous Neighborhoods

There has long been interest in how the attributes of neighborhoods and communities affect human motivation and patterns of behavior, with particular concerns on how living in dilapidated and dangerous neighborhoods might negatively impact children and adults (Leventhal & Brooks-Gunn, 2000; Minh et al., 2017; Rollings et al., 2017). Residents in communities with abandoned or ruined buildings are often socially isolated and report higher levels of incivilities (Jaskiewicz & Wiwatowska, 2018; Reisig & Cancino, 2004). Living in a dangerous or rundown neighborhood contributes to parenting stress; and, as a consequence, it reduces parental expressions of warmth and increases punitiveness (Aisenberg & Ell, 2005; Cuellar et al., 2015). Not surprisingly, parents living in dangerous areas tend to increase the amount of monitoring (Jones et al., 2002; Vieno et al., 2010). However, the findings are mixed, with some evidence that the influence is greater for low-income families and immigrant families with low levels of acculturation (Barnett et al., 2016; Cueller et al, 2015; Kohen et al., 2008).

Blighted neighborhoods can pose substantial risk for childhood injury and diminished health. Both indoor and outdoor contaminants are more prevalent in rundown areas of town, especially in inner-city areas of large urban environments. Prenatal exposure to air particulates appears to cause disruptions in the endocrine system's processes and can lead to growth retardation, prematurity, and birth defects (Dadvand et al., 2013). Early exposure to pollutants can have negative consequences for the central nervous system and cognitive functions (Cowell et al., 2019; Rivas et al., 2019); and it increases the likelihood a child will have respiratory tract illnesses and ear infections (Aguilera et al., 2013; Wang, 2019). As children get older and are allowed to wander (unsupervised) into the neighborhood, injuries are also more likely (Bradley, Corwyn, Burchinal et al., 2001; Dercon & Krishnam, 2009). Although the dangers present in poor rural areas and poor urban areas are somewhat different, the broad dangers they present likely motivate rural parents to take some of the same precautions with respect to child monitoring and behavior control as is the case with parents living in urban slums (Ramirez & Villarejo, 2012)

Area of residence can be a factor in how often parents engage their children in outdoor physical activity or whether parents will allow children to engage in outdoor physical activity on their own, leading to better overall fitness for children (Dunton et al., 2014; Kaczynski & Henderson, 2007; Zaltauske & Petrauskiene, 2016). As expected, living in densely populated, inner-city neighborhoods, particularly those with poor physical amenities and high concentrations of poor families, can discourage outdoor activities (Brockman et al., 2011; Tigges et al., 1998). It is part of a larger tendency to be more restrictive with children (Jones et al., 2005; O'Neil et al., 2001; Vieno et al., 2010). Thus, it is not surprising that parents in neighborhoods with high levels of disorder tend not to take their children out to play even when parks are readily available for use (Miles, 2008).

Living in a poor neighborhood decreases the odds children will receive potentially enriching lessons or visit libraries and museums (Cueller et al., 2015). Living in dilapidated neighborhoods, where social cohesion tends to be low, parents tend not to form strong social ties with neighbors or let their children go out to play with neighborhood children either, thus reducing the children's opportunities for developing social skills and to become socially integrated into the community (Kohen et al., 2008; Parcel & Bixby, 2016).

Although the research on "neighborhood effects" is growing, it is critical not to overplay the findings, particularly since parental characteristics have a bearing on where a family resides and findings are somewhat inconsistent (Cueller et al., 2015; Minh et al., 2017). Moreover, the negative effects generally observed do not equally apply to all groups; that is, there appear to be both parent characteristics and contextual conditions that reduce the impact of living in a rundown neighborhood (Sharkey & Faber, 2014). Because neighborhoods are such dynamic, complex entities, it can be difficult to determine just how some aspect of the overall neighborhood matters for children, thus the need for studies that examine multiple mechanisms and potential moderators in an integrative way.

7.5 Lower- and Middle-Income Countries (LMICs)

Since its founding, UNICEF has focused on areas of the world that are politically fragmented and resource-poor, conditions often present in LMICs (UNICEF, 2020). In LMICs, families often reside in houses that are poorly constructed and that have few amenities; and families also often live in neighborhoods and communities that have few amenities (Bain et al., 2014; Bornstein et al., 2015; WHO, 2018, 2019). People in LMICs often have less access to safe drinking water, good nutrition, and adequate sanitation facilities (McMichael, 2019; UNICEF, 2019). Residents in LMICS are at increased risk of exposure to toxicants as well, including exposure to high levels of air and water pollution if they live in high-density urban areas (Suk et al., 2016). These conditions pose threats to overall well-being for children and adults (Boyle et al., 2006; Bradley & Putnick, 2016; Dercon & Krishnan, 2009; McEniry, 2013; WHO, 2018). A report released in 2016 by UNICEF indicated that rates of child mortality remain high in LMICs and that 40 percent of children in LMICs will leave primary school unable to read, write, or do basic arithmetic.

The UN, WHO, and World Bank advocate for "enabling environments" (i.e., environments that contain sufficient material and social resources to facilitate human competence). Access to an enabling environment is important for parents, as they must meet not only their own needs but also the needs of their children. There is scarce research on how specific types of assets at the country level affect parenting. However, studies show that parents in LMICS tend to provide lower levels of stimulation and socioemotional support to their children than is deemed desirable by professionals (Black et al., 2016; Bornstein et al., 2015; Sun et al., 2016; Walker et al., 2007).

Life is not the same for all who reside in LMICs. Where one lives in an LMIC can affect the prospect one will experience multidimensional poverty and the increased vulnerability that typically accompanies it. Families living in rural areas in LMICs face numerous overlapping structural constraints to their health and adaptive functioning (Strasser, 2003). For those who depend on agriculture for a livelihood, managing daily tasks can be difficult due to seasonal unemployment and low wages (United Nations Development Program, 2014). In such families, children frequently help with daily activities; thus, children are less likely to have opportunities for continuing their education (Food and Agriculture Organization of the United Nations, 2017). Pervasive poverty in rural areas, together with isolation of residents and lack of social resources and physical infrastructure, leads to social exclusion for many (European Commission, 2008).

For many who reside in LMICs, life can be daunting. In a study done in forty-two developing countries, Boyle and colleagues (2006) observed shared variation in country-level wealth, family-level wealth, and maternal education. Although research does not make fully clear how simultaneous exposure to individual and aggregate poverty affects parenting, it appears highly likely that having few resources to draw upon would leave both children and adults quite vulnerable (Calvo & Dercon, 2013).

7.6 Parent Mental Illness and Substance Abuse

Among the most significant challenges a child can face is living with a parent who has mental health or substance abuse problems, especially if both parents face such problems (Dietz et al., 2009; Kahn et al., 2004; Simpson-Adkins & Daiches, 2018; Solis et al., 2012). As was addressed to some degree in Section 6 on caregiving processes, parents with mental illness and substance abuse problems are less likely to provide a child with the full array of supports needed for optimal development (Lander et al., 2013; National Research Council & Institute of Medicine, 2009).

7.6.1 Mental Illness

Struggling with mental illness can make it difficult for parents to engage fully in caring for their children (Thomas & Kalucy, 2003). In some cases, the relationship between parent and child switches so that the child becomes caregiver (Aldridge, 2006). Oyserman and colleagues (2000) found that children whose parents had mental illness manifest a diverse array of developmental problems, beginning with insecure attachment as infants. Not surprisingly, during episodes of mental illness, parents were less likely to afford their offspring sensitive care, to provide consistent discipline, to engage their children in stimulating joint activity, to productively communicate with their children, or to carefully monitor offspring (Frank & Meara, 2009; Koblinsky et al., 2006). Somewhat different patterns of behavior have been observed in parents with different types of mental illness (Reupert et al., 2012). Moreover, the specific behaviors observed varied as a consequence of other contextual factors (e.g., single-parent status, level of social support available, household income); and parental behavior varied as a consequence of the persistence of psychiatric problem (Letourneau et al., 2010; Reupert et al., 2012).

Although research on mental illness in parents and how it affects children has limitations, findings are fairly clear in showing that the children face a myriad of challenges. In some cases, parents lose custody of a child (Kohl et al., 2011). As a consequence, many of the children manifest poor health, diminished competence, and maladaptive behavior (Hameed & Lewis, 2016; Siegenthaler et al., 2012).

7.6.2 Substance Abuse

When mothers consume alcohol or drugs during pregnancy, it can lead to a diverse array of developmental problems, including fetal alcohol syndrome, poor cognitive and language development, emotion dysregulation, and electroencephalographic abnormalities (Johnson & Leff, 1999; Ross et al., 2015; Smith et al., 2016). When parents abuse alcohol and drugs, it creates conditions that can lead to child maltreatment (US Department of Health and Human Services, 2019), with persistent substance abuse often resulting in a child being removed from the home (Lander et al., 2013). For the child, this can lead to feelings of loss and abandonment and to a deep sense of uncertainty. Various forms of maltreatment, from neglect to traumatic victimization, can make it difficult for children to regulate their emotions. It can also lead to hyperarousal, lower levels of competence, and difficulties establishing healthy boundaries in relationships (Johnson & Leff, 1999; Zucker et al., 2009).

Research on many particular substances is limited. Even so, it suggests that the impacts on children vary somewhat by type of substance and the nature and timing of exposure. For example, a meta-analysis of prenatal opioid exposure indicated that there were long-term impacts on both cognitive and motor development (Yeoh et al., 2019). By comparison, a review of studies on parents' postnatal use of opioids showed negative impacts on the parent–child relationship and on children's adaptive behavior, partly reflecting more negative behavior toward the child (Romanowicz et al., 2019). It is difficult to separate the genetic and environmental influences on various outcomes. Moreover, not all children living with parents who have substance abuse problems manifest serious developmental problems. When families can remain relatively cohesive and children perceive that they have social support, children can be relatively resilient despite their parents' use of substances, partly because they retain a sense of belonging (El-Sheikh & Buckhalt, 2003; Lee & Williams, 2013; Wlodarczyk et al., 2017).

The challenges presented by parents with mental illness and parents with substance abuse problems can quickly multiply, especially when families are poor and experience high levels of instability (Lander et al., 2013). These conditions increase the likelihood of poorer-quality parenting and poor outcomes for children. However, as stated, the outcomes at parent, child, and family levels are quite diverse. A major factor in determining how children respond to inadequate parenting and poor household conditions is the child's own skills and proclivities. Children who are brighter and who have more social skills tend to fare better (Radke-Yarrow & Sherman, 1990), for example. It is also the case that children with one parent who struggles with mental illness or substance abuse problems can be protected to some degree if there is a second parent who provides stability and nurturant care (Chang et al., 2007).

In evaluating research on contextual challenges, it is important not to interpret findings in ways that disparage parents or children. Many of the challenges reflect systemic problems rather than individual deficiencies. There is a rapidly expanding literature on how discrimination at many levels affects where people live, how they are treated, and the opportunities they have for optimal development (Becares et al., 2015; Trent et al., 2019). In addition, there is a literature on resilience that makes clear that many children and adults who face particular challenges deal with those challenges in ways that are quite productive for themselves and others (Aburn et al., 2016). These bodies of research point the way to new lines of inquiry and new policies and programs for families that face challenges.

8 The Times, They Are a' Changin' – and So Are We

As addressed in Section 5, life is vastly different today than a century ago; and it vaguely resembles life prior to the establishment of agriculture. The concentration of people in dense urban centers, the penetration of media into almost every aspect of daily life, and advances in smart technologies and robotics are only part of the sea of adjustments in human life that have occurred. Life is changing in LMICs as well as technologically advanced countries – granted most of the research discussed in this overview has been done in technologically advanced countries. Thus, there is a need for concerted attention to how aspects of the environment in LMICs impact the lives of children (Black et al., 2017).

Combining the principles articulated in ecological-developmental theory and dynamic systems theory, one would expect that the rapid evolution in human life will lead to changes in the interplay between various contextual aspects of family life and how they influence parent behavior, parent–child relationships, and child development. The evolution in human life is also likely to change how parent behavior is organized in and through time and how interactions between children and parents are organized in and through time. Perhaps most critically, the evolution is likely to change how these behaviors influence children's developmental course. Far more research is needed on how parent and child behavior changes as children age and as a function of different contexts. Otherwise, it will be difficult to fashion effective training programs and policies that have benefits for children and their caregivers (Perrin et al., 2016).

Over the passage of time, historians, archeologists, artists, religious leaders, and scientists have noted – in their own ways – that there is more to the universe than we suspected. Numerous mysteries remain in how the environment is implicated in children's development. New technologies, new approaches to analyzing data, and new theories may help in gradually unraveling the nature of the relation between children's environments and their life outcomes.

References

Aaron, R. F., & Witt, P. A. (2011). Urban students' definitions and perceptions of nature. *Children, Youth and Environments*, *21*, 145–167.

Ablewhite, J., McDaid, L., Hawkins, A. et al. (2015). Approaches used by parents to keep their children safe at home: A qualitative study to explore the perspectives of parents with children under five years. *BMC Public Health*, *15*, 983.

Aburn, G., Gott, M., & Hoare, K. (2016). What is resilience: An integrative review of the empirical literature. *Journal of Advanced Nursing*, *72*, 980–1000.

Agrawal, P., & Gulati, J. (2005). The patterns of infant-mother attachment as a function of home environment. *Journal of Human Ecology*, *18*, 287–293.

Aguilera, I., Pedersen, M., Garcia-Esteban, R. et al. (2013). Early life exposure to outdoor air pollution and respiratory health, ear infections, and eczema in infants from the INMA study. *Environmental Health Perspectives*, *121*, 387–392.

Aisenberg, E., & Ell, K. (2005). Contextualizing community violence and its effects: An ecological model of parent-child interdependent coping. *Journal of Interpersonal Violence*, *20*, 855–871.

Aldridge, J. (2006). The experiences of children living with and caring for parents with mental illness. *Child Abuse Review*, *15*, 79–88.

Allcott, H. D, Diamond, R., Handbury, J. P. et al. (2019). Food deserts and the causes of nutritional inequality. *Quarterly Journal of Economics*, *134*, 1793–1844.

American Academy of Pediatrics. (2016). Recommendations for preventive pediatric health care. *Pediatrics*, *137*: e20153908.

American College of Pediatricians. (2016). *The Impact of Media Use and Screen Time on Children, Adolescents and Families*, November. www .acpeds.org/the-college-speaks/position-statements/parenting-issues/the-impact-of-media-use-and-screen-time-on-children-adolescents-and-families

American Psychological Association. (2008). *Presidential Task Force on Posttraumatic Stress Disorder and Trauma in Children and Adolescents Children and Trauma: Update for Mental Health Professionals*. Washington, DC: American Psychological Association.

Anderson, S. E., & Whitaker, R. C. (2010). Household routines and obesity in US preschool-aged children. *Pediatrics*, *125*, 420–428.

Assari, S. (2013). Race, ethnicity, religion involvement, church-based social support and subjective health in the United States: A case of moderated-mediation. *International Journal of Preventive Medicine, 4,* 208–217.

Association of Science-Technology Centers. (2014). *2013 Science Center and Museum Statistics.* www.astc.org/wp-content/uploads/2014/10/2013-Science-Center-Statistics.pdf

Atkin, A. J., Sharp, S. J., Harrison, F. et al. (2016). Seasonal variation in children's physical activity and sedentary time. *Medical Science and Sports Exercise, 48,* 449–456.

Avants, B. B., Hackman, D. A., Betancourt, L. M. et al. (2015). Relation of childhood home environment to cortical thickness in late adolescence: Specificity of experience and timing. *PLoS ONE 10,* e0138217.

Awasthi, S., Glick, H. A., & Fletcher, R. H. (1996). Effect of cooking fuels on respiratory diseases in preschool children in Lucknow, India. *American Journal of Tropical Medicine and Hygiene, 55,* 48–51.

Aziz, N. F., & Said, I. (2012). The trends and influential factors of children's use of outdoor environments: A review. *Procedia: Social and Behavioral Sciences, 38,* 204–212.

Babisch, W., Neuhauser, H., Thamm, M. et al. (2009). Blood pressure of 8–14 year old children in relation to traffic noise at home: Results of the German Environmental Survey for Children (GerES IV). *Science of the Total Environment, 407,* 5839–5043.

Bain, R., Cronk, R., Wright, J. et al. (2014). Fecal contamination of drinking water in low- and middle-income countries: A systematic review and meta-analysis. *PLoS Medicine, 11*(5): e1001644.

Baker, C. E. (2013). Fathers' and mothers' home literacy involvement and children's cognitive and social emotional development: Implications for family literacy programs. *Applied Developmental Science, 117,* 184–197.

Banyard, V. L., Williams, L., & Siegel, J. (2003). The impact of complex trauma and depression on parenting: An exploration of mediating risk and protective factors. *Child Maltreatment, 8,* 334–349.

Barajas, M. S. (2011). Academic achievement of children in single parent homes: A critical review. *The Hilltop Review, 5,* 13–21.

Barker, J. E., Semenov, A. D. Michaelson, L. et al. (2014). Less-structured time in children's daily lives predicts self-directed executive functioning. *Frontiers in Psychology, 5,* 503.

Barkin, S., Ip, E., & Richardson, I. (2006). Parental mediation style for children aged 2 to 11 years. *Archives of Pediatrics and Adolescent Medicine, 160,* 395–401.

Barnard, M., & McKeganey, N. (2004). The impact of parental problem drug use on children: What is the problem and what can be done to help? *Addiction, 99*, 552–559.

Barnett, M. A., Mills-Koonce, W. R., Gustafsson, H. et al. (2012). Mother-grandmother conflict, negative parenting and young children's social development in multigenerational families. *Family Relations, 61*, 864–877.

Barnett, M. A., Mortensen, J. A., Gonzalez, H., & Gonzalez, J. (2016). Cultural factors moderating links between neighborhood disadvantage and parenting and coparenting among Mexican origin families. *Child and Youth Care Forum, 45*, 927–845.

Barr, R. (2013). Memory constraints on infant learning from picture books, television, and touchscreens. *Child Development Perspectives, 7*, 205–210.

Bartlett, S. (1999). Children's experience of the physical environment in poor urban settlements and the implications for policy and practice. *Environment and Urbanization, 11*, 63–73.

Bavelier, D., Green, C. S., & Dye, M. W. (2010). Children wired: For better and for worse. *Neuron, 67*, 692–701.

Becares, L., Nazroo, J., & Kelly, Y. (2015). A longitudinal examination of maternal, family, and area-level experiences of racism on children's socio-emotional development: Patterns and possible explanations. *Social Science and Medicine, 142*, 128–135.

Beck, B., Butter, A., Jr., & Lennon, M. C. (2016). Home moves and child wellbeing in the first five years of life in the United States. *Longitudinal and Life Course Studies, 7*, 240–264.

Belanger, H., & Coolen, H. (2014). *Affordance and Behavior Setting: A Multi-level Ecological Perspective in the Study of the Meaning of Habitat.* www.semanticscholar.org/paper/Affordance-and-behavior-setting%3A-A-multi-level-in-B%C3%A9langer-Coolen/2d01b2e738e601c957c565fab268543a1b6100bf

Belle, D. (1999). *The After-School Lives of Children: Alone and with Others While Parents Work.* Mahwah, NJ: Lawrence Erlbaum Associates.

Belsky, J., Putnam, S., & Crnic, K. (1997). Coparenting, parenting, and early emotional development. *New Directions in Child Development, 74*, 45–56.

Bento, G, & Dias, G. (2017). The importance of outdoor play for young children's healthy development. *Porto Biomedical Journal, 2*, 157–160.

Besson, A. (2017). Building a paradise? On the quest for the optimal human habitat. *Contemporary Aesthetics, 17*, 806.

Biedinger, N. (2011). The influence of education and home environment on the cognitive outcomes of preschool children in Germany. *Child Development Research*, https://doi.org/10.1155/2011/916303

Bjorklund, D., Hubertz, M., & Reubens, A. (2004). Young children's arithmetic strategies in social context: How parents contribute to children's strategy development while playing games. *International Journal of Behavioral Development, 28*, 347–357.

Black, M. M., Fernandez-Rao, S., Hurley, K. et al. (2016). Growth and development among infants and preschoolers in rural India: Economic inequities and caregiver protective/promotive factors. *International Journal of Behavioral Development, 40*, 526–535.

Black, M. M., Perez-Escamilla, R., & Rao, S. F. (2015). Integrating nutrition and child development interventions: Scientific basis, evidence of impact, and implementation considerations. *Advances in Nutrition, 6*, 852–859.

Black, M. M., Walker, S. P., Fernald, L. C. et al. (2017). Advancing early childhood development: From science to scale: 1. *Lancet, 389*, 77–90.

Blair, C., & Raver, C. C. (2012). Child development in the context of adversity. *American Psychologist, 67*, 309–318.

Blewitt, P., Rump, K., Shealy, S. et al. (2009). Shared book reading: When and how questions affect young children's word learning. *Journal of Educational Psychology, 101*, 294–304.

Blumberg, F. C., Deater-Deckard, K., Calvert, S. L. et al. (2019). Digital games as a context for children's cognitive development: Research recommendations and policy considerations. *SRCD Social Policy Report, 32*, 1–21.

Bonney, J. F., Kelley, M. L., & Levant, R. F. (1999). A model of fathers' behavioral involvement in child care in dual-earner families. *Journal of Family Psychology, 13*, 401–415.

Bornstein, M. H. (2015). Determinants of parenting. In D. Cicchetti (Ed.), *Developmental Psychopathology*, vol. 4 (3rd ed., pp. 180–270). Hoboken, NJ: John Wiley.

Bornstein, M. H. (2017). The specificity principle in acculturation science. *Psychological Science, 12*, 3–45.

Bornstein, M. H., & Manian, N. (2013). Maternal responsiveness and sensitivity reconsidered: Some is more. *Development and Psychopathology, 25*, 957–971.

Bornstein, M. H., Putnick, D. L., Bradley, R. H. et al. (2015). Pathways among caregiver education, household resources, and infant growth in 39 low- and middle-income countries. *Infancy, 20*, 353–376.

Boursnell, M. (2014). Assessing the capacity of parents with mental illness: Parents with mental illness and risk. *International Social Work, 7*, 92–108.

Bowlby, J. (1969). *Attachment and Loss, Vol. 1: Attachment*. New York: Basic Books.

Boyce, W. T., Sokolowski, M. B., & Robinson, G. E. (2013). Toward a biology of social adversity. *PNAS, 109* (Suppl. 2), 17143–17148.

Boyle, M. H., Racine, Y., Georgiades, K. et al. (2006). The influence of economic development level, household wealth and maternal education on child health in the developing world. *Social Science and Medicine, 63,* 2242–2254.

Bradley, R. H. (2006). Home environment. In N. Watt, C. Ayoub, R. H. Bradley, J. Puma, & W. LaBoeuf (Eds.), *The Crisis in Youth Mental Health, Vol. 4: Early Intervention Programs and Policies* (pp. 89–120). Westport, CT: Greenwood Publishing Group.

Bradley, R. H. (2012). Rural versus urban environments. In L. C. Mayes & M. Lewis (Eds.), *A Developmental Environment Measurement Handbook* (pp. 330–346). New York: Cambridge University Press.

Bradley, R. H. (2017). Social and contextual risks. In E. Vortruba-Drzal & E. Dearing (Eds.), *Handbook of Early Childhood Development Programs, Practices, and Policies: Theoretically and Empirically-Supported Strategies for Promoting Young Children's Growth in the United States* (pp. 66–97). Hoboken, NJ: Wiley.

Bradley, R. H., & Caldwell, B. M. (1984a). The HOME inventory and family demographics. *Developmental Psychology, 20,* 315–320.

Bradley, R. H., & Caldwell, B. M. (1984b). The relation of infants' home environments to achievement test performance in first grade: A follow-up study. *Child, Development, 55,* 803–809.

Bradley, R. H., Corwyn, R. F., Burchinal, M. et al. (2001). The home environments of children in the United States. Part 2: Relations with behavioral development through age 13. *Child Development, 72,* 1868–1886.

Bradley, R. H., Corwyn, R. F., McAdoo, H. P. et al. (2001). The home environments of children in the United States. Part 1: Variations by age, ethnicity, and poverty status. *Child Development, 72,* 1844–1867.

Bradley, R. H., & Putnick, D. L. (2012). Housing quality and access to material and learning resources within the home environment in developing countries. *Child Development, 83,* 76–91.

Bradley, R. H., & Putnick, D. L. (2016). The role of physical capital assets in young girls' and boys' mortality and growth in low- and middle-income countries. *Monographs of the Society for Research in Child Development, 81,* 33–59.

Bradley, R. H., Whiteside, L., Mundfrom, D. J. et al. (1994). Early indications of resilience and their relation to experiences in the home environments of low birthweight, premature children living in poverty. *Child Development, 65,* 246–260.

Brannon, D., & Daukas, L. (2014). The effectiveness of dialogic reading in increasing English language learning preschool children's expressive language. *International Research in Early Childhood Education, 5,* 1–10

Bransford, J. D., Brown, A. L., & Cocking, R. R. (2000). *How People Learn: Brain, Mind, Experience, and School.* Washington, DC: The National Academies Press.

Brenner, R. A., & the Committee on Injury, Violence, and Poison Prevention. (2003). Prevention of drowning in infants, children, and adolescents. *Pediatrics, 112,* 440–445.

Bretherton, I., & Waters, E. (1985). Growing points of attachment theory. *Monographs of the Society for Research in Child Development, 50*(209).

Briggs, S., Cantrell, E., & Kkarberg, E. (2019). *Family Instability and Children's Social Development.* Child Trends brief. www.childtrends.org /publications/family-instability-and-childrens-social-development

Brockman, R., Jago, R., & Fox, K R. (2011). Children's active play: Self-reported motivators, barriers and facilitators. *BMC Public Health, 11,* 461.

Bronson, M. B. (2000). *Self-Regulation in Early Childhood.* New York: Guilford Press.

Brooks-Gunn, J., & Donahue, E. H. (2008). Introducing the issue. *The Future of Children, 18,* 3–10.

Brumbaugh, J. E., Hansen, N. I., Bell, E. F. et al. (2019). Outcomes of extremely preterm infants with birth weight less than 400g. *JAMA Pediatrics, 173,* 434–445

Bruner, J. (1983). *Child Talk: Learning to Use Language.* Oxford: Oxford University Press.

Burlaka, V., Kim, Y. J., Crutchfield, J. M. et al. (2017). Predictors of internalizing behaviors in Ukrainian children. *Family Relations, 66,* 854–866.

Burnette, C. E., & Figley, C. R. (2016). Risk and protective factors related to the wellness of American Indian and Alaska Native youth: A systematic review. *International Public Health Journal, 8,* 137–154.

Cabrera, N., Hofferth, S., & Soo, C. (2011). Patterns and predictors of father-infant engagement across race/ethnic groups. *Early Childhood Research Quarterly, 26,* 365–375.

Calvo, C., & Dercon, S. (2013). Vulnerability to individual and aggregate poverty. *Social Choice and Welfare, 41,* 721–740.

Cameron-Faulkner, T., Melville, J., & Gattis, M. (2018). Responding to nature: Natural environments improve parent-child communication. *Journal of Environmental Psychology, 59,* 9–15.

Carver, C. S., & Conner-Smith, J. (2010). Personality and coping. *Annual Review of Psychology*, *61*, 679–704.

Casey, J. A., Morello-Frosch, R., Mennitt, D. J. et al. (2017). Race/ethnicity, socioeconomic status residential segregation, and spatial variation in noise exposure in the contiguous United States. *Environmental Health Perspectives*, *125*, 077017.

Cavanagh, S. E., & Huston, A. C. (2006). Family instability and children's early problem behavior. *Social Forces*, *85*, 551–582.

Ceballo, R., & McLoyd, V. C. (2002). Social support and parenting in poor, dangerous neighborhoods. *Child Development*, *73*, 1310–1321.

Centers for Disease Control. (2015). *10 Leading Causes of Death by Age Group, United States – 2014*. www.cdc.gov/injury/wisqars/pdf/leading_causes_of_death_by_age_group_2014-a.pdf

Chang, J. J., Halpern, C. T., & Kaufman, J. S. (2007). Maternal depressive symptoms, father's involvement, and the trajectories of child problem behaviors in a US national sample. *Archives of Pediatrics and Adolescent Medicine*, *161*, 697–703.

Chao, R., & Kanatsu, A. (2008). Beyond socioeconomics: Explaining ethnic group differences in parenting through cultural and immigration processes. *Applied Developmental Science*, *12*, 181–187.

Chassiakos, Y., Radesky, J., Christakis, D. et al. (2016). Children and adolescents and digital media. *Pediatrics*, *138*, e20162593.

Chemero, A. (2009). *Radical Embodied Cognitive Science*. Cambridge, MA: MIT Press.

Chen, E., Cohen, S., & Miller, G. E. (2010). How low socioeconomic status affects 2-year hormonal trajectories in children. *Psychological Science*, *21*, 31–37.

Child Trends. (2015). *Participation in School Music and Other Performing Arts, Indicators on Children and Youth*. www.childtrends.org/wp-content/uploads/2015/11/36_Participation_in_Performing_Arts1.pdf

Christakis, D. A., Ramirez, J. S, & Ramirez, J. M. (2012). Overstimulation of newborn mice leads to behavioral differences and deficits in cognitive performance. *Scientific Reports*, *2*, 546.

Clair, A. (2019). Housing: An under-explored influence on children's well-being and becoming. *Child Indicators Research*, *12*, 609–626.

Cohen, G. L., & Sherman, D. K. (2014). The psychology of change: Self-affirmation and social psychology intervention. *Annual Review of Psychology*, *65*, 333–371.

Coldwell, J., Pike, A., & Dunn, J. (2006). Household chaos: Links with parenting and child behavior. *Journal of Child Psychology and Psychiatry*, *47*, 1116–1122.

Coley, R. L., Leventhal, T., Lynch, A. D. et al. (2013). Relations between housing characteristics and well-being of low-income children and adolescents. *Developmental Psychology*, *49*, 1775–1789.

Conger, R. D., Conger, K. J., & Martin, M. J. (2010). Socioeconomic status, family processes, and child development. *Journal of Marriage and Family*, *72*, 685–704.

Corapci, F., & Wachs, T. (2002). Does parental mood or efficacy mediate the influence of environmental chaos on parenting behavior? *Merrill-Palmer Quarterly*, *48*, 182–201.

Corrigall, K., & Schellenberg, E. G. (2015). Predicting who takes music lessons: Parent and child characteristics. *Frontiers in Psychology*, *6*, 282.

Cowell, W. J., Brunst, K. J., Malin, A. J. et al. (2019). Prenatal exposure to PM2.5 and cardiac vagal tone during infancy: Findings from a multiethnic birth cohort. *Environmental Health Perspectives*, 127, 4434. https://doi.org/10.1289/EHP4434

Cox, A. M. (2018). Space and embodiment in informal learning. *Higher Education*, *75*, 1077–1090.

Cox, A., Loebach, J., & Little, S. (2018). Understanding the nature play milieu: Behavior mapping to investigate children's activities in outdoor play spaces. *Children, Youth and Environment*, *28*, 232–261.

Coyne, S. M., Radesky, J., Collier, K. M. et al. (2017). Parenting and digital media. *Pediatrics*, *140*, S112.

Craig, L., Powell, A., & Smyth, C. (2014). Towards intensive parenting? Changes in the composition and determinants of mothers' and fathers' time with children 1992–2006. *British Journal of Sociology*, *65*, 555–579.

Crespi, I. (2014). Foreign families in the Italian context: Migration processes and strategies. *Journal of Comparative Family Studies*, *45*, 249–260.

Criss, M. M., Shaw, D. S., & Ingolsby, E. M. (2003). Mother-son positive synchrony in middle childhood: Relations to antisocial behavior. *Social Development*, *12*, 379–400.

Crosnoe, R., & Muller, C. (2014). Family socioeconomic status, peers, and the path to college. *Social Problems*, *61*, 602–624.

Crosnoe, R., Prickett, K. C., Smith, C. et al. (2014). Changes in young children's family structures and child care arrangements. *Demography*, *51*, 459–483.

Crouch, E., Radcliff, E., Probst, J. C. et al. (2019). Rural-urban differences in adverse childhood experiences across a national sample of children. *Journal of Rural Health*, *36*, 55–64.

Cuellar, J., Jones, D. J., & Sterrett, E. (2015). Examining parenting in neighborhood context: A review. *Journal of Child and Family Studies*, *24*, 195–219.

Cummings, E. M., & Davies, P. T. (2002). Effects of marital conflict on children: Recent advances and emerging themes in process-oriented research. *Journal of Child Psychology and Psychiatry, 43*, 31–63.

Cunha, F., & Heckman, J. (2007). The technology of skill formation. *American Economic Review, 97*, 31–47.

Curry, K. A., Jean-Marie, G., & Adams, C. M. (2016). Social networks and parent motivational beliefs: Evidence from an urban school district. *Educational Administration Quarterly, 52*, 841–877.

Dadvand, P., Parher, J., Bell, M. et al. (2013). Maternal exposure to particulate air pollution and term birth weight: A multi-country evaluation of effect and heterogeneity. *Environmental Health Perspectives, 121*, 367–373.

Dadvand, P., Pujol, J., Macià, D. et al. (2018). The association between lifelong greenspace exposure and 3-dimensional brain magnetic resonance imaging in Barcelona schoolchildren. *Environmental Health Perspectives 126*, 027012

Dadvand, P., Tischer, C., Estarlich, M. et al. (2017). Lifelong residential exposure to green space and attention: A population perspective study. *Environmental Health Perspectives, 125*, 694.

Dearing, E., Casey, B., Ganley, C. et al. (2012). Young girls' arithmetic and spatial skills: The distal and proximal roles of family socioeconomics and home learning experiences. *Early Childhood Research Quarterly, 27*, 4458–470.

De Bellis, M. D., & Zisk, A. (2014). The biological effects of childhood trauma. *Child and Adolescent Psychiatric Clinics of North America, 23*, 185–222.

Delamater, P. L., Messina, J. P., Shortridge, A. M. et al. (2012). Measuring geographic access to health care: Raster and network-based models. *International Journal of Health Geographics, 11*, 15.

De Lisi, R., & Wolford, J. (2002). Improving children's mental rotation accuracy with computer games. *Journal of Genetic Psychology, 163*, 272–282.

DeLoache, J. S., Chiong, C., Sherman, K. et al. (2010). Do babies learn from baby media? *Psychological Science, 21*, 1570–1574.

Dercon, S., & Krishnan, P. (2009). Poverty and the psychosocial competencies of children: Evidence from the Young Lives sample in four developing countries. *Children, Youth and Environments, 19*, 138–163.

De Silva, M. J., & Harpham, T. (2007). Maternal social capital and child nutritional status in four developing countries. *Health and Place, 13*, 341–455.

Desmond, M., & Kimbro, R. T. (2016). Eviction's fallout: Housing, hardship, and health. *Social Forces, 94*, 295–324.

Dettmers, S., Yotyodying, S., & Jonkmann, K. (2019). Antecedents and outcomes of parental homework involvement: How do family-school partnerships affect parental homework involvement and student outcomes? *Frontiers in Psychology, 10,* 1048.

Dietz, L., Jennings, K. D., Kelley, S. A. et al. (2009). Maternal depression, paternal psychopathology, and toddlers' behavior problems. *Journal of Clinical Child and Adolescent Psychology, 39,* 48–61.

Ding, D., Sallis, J. F., Kerr, J. et al. (2011). Neighborhood environment and physical activity among youth. *American Journal of Preventive Medicine, 41,* 442–455.

Donovan, L., & Brown, M. (2017). *Leveraging Change: Increasing Access to Arts Education in Rural America.* www.giarts.org/sites/default/files/leveraging-change-increasing-access-arts-education-rural-areas.pdf

Drotar, D. (1985). *New Directions in Failure-to-Thrive: Research and Clinical Practice.* New York: Plenum.

Dumas, J., Nissley, J., Nordstrom, A. et al. (2005). Home chaos: Sociodemographic, parenting, interactional, and child correlates. *Journal of Child and Adolescent Psychology, 34,* 93–104.

Dunifon, R., & Bairacharya, A. (2012). The role of grandparents in the lives of youth. *Journal of Family Issues, 33,* 1168–1194.

Dunn, J., & Brown, J. (1994). Affect expression in the family, Children's understanding of emotions and their interactions with others. *Merrill-Palmer Quarterly, 40,* 120–137.

Dunton, G. F., Almanza, E., Jerrett, M. et al. (2014). Neighborhood park use by children: Use of accelerometry and global positioning systems. *American Journal of Preventive Medicine, 46,* 136–142.

Dush, C. M., Schmeer, K. K., & Taylor, M. (2013). Chaos as a social determinant of child health: Reciprocal associations? *Social Science and Medicine, 95,* 69–76.

Easterlin, R. A., Angelescu, L., & Zweig, J. S. (2011). The impact of modern economic growth on urban-rural differences in subjective well-being. *World Development, 39,* 2187–2198.

Egger, H. L, & Angold, A. (2006). Common emotional and behavioral disorders in preschool children: presentation, nosology, and epidemiology. *Journal of Child Psychology and Psychiatry, 47,* 313–337.

Eime, R. M., Charity, M. J., Harvey, J. T. et al. (2015). Participation in sport and physical activity: Associations with socio-economic status and geographical remoteness. *BMC Public Health, 15,* 434.

El-Sheikh, M., & Buckhalt, J. A. (2003). Parental problem drinking and children's adjustment: attachment and family functioning as moderators and mediators of risk. *Journal of Family Psychology, 4,* 510–520.

European Commission. (2008). *Poverty and Social Exclusion in Rural Areas. Final Report.* ec.europa.eu/social/BlobServlet?docId=2087&langId=en

Evans, G. W. (2006). Child development and the physical environment. *Annual Review of Psychology, 57,* 423–451.

Evans, G. W., Bullinger, M., & Hygge, S. (1998). Chronic noise exposure and physiological response: A prospective, longitudinal study of children under environmental stress. *Psychological Science, 9,* 75–77.

Evans, G. W., Gonnella, C., Marcynyszyn, L. et al. (2005). The role of chaos in poverty and children's socioemotional adjustment. *Psychological Science, 16,* 560–565.

Evans, G. W., & Kim, P. (2013). Childhood poverty, chronic stress, self-regulation and coping. *Child Development Perspectives, 7,* 43–48.

Evans, G. W., Li, D., & Whipple, S. S. (2013). Cumulative risk and child development. *Psychological Bulletin, 139,* 1342–1396.

Evans, G. W., Maxwell, L., & Hart, B. (1999). Parental language and verbal responsiveness to children in crowded homes. *Developmental Psychology, 35,* 1020–1023.

Evans, G. W., Riccuitti, H. N., Hope, S. et al. (2010). Crowding and cognitive development. The mediating role of maternal responsiveness among 36-month-old children. *Environment & Behavior, 42,* 135–148.

Evans, G. W., & Wachs, T. D. (2010). *Chaos and Its Influence on Children's Development: An Ecological Perspective.* Washington, DC: American Psychological Association.

Ezeh, K., Agho, K. E., Dibley, M. J. (2014). The impact of water and sanitation on childhood mortality in Nigeria: Evidence from demographic and health surveys, 2003–2013. *International Journal of Environmental Research in Public Health, 11,* 92d56–9272.

Fakhouri, T. H., Hughes, J. P., Brody, D. J. et al. (2013). Physical activity and screen-time viewing among elementary school-aged children in the United States from 2009 to 2010. *JAMA Pediatrics, 167,* 2230229.

Farver, J. A., Xu, Y., Eppe, S. et al. (2006). Home environments and young Latino children's school readiness. *Early Childhood Research Quarterly, 21,* 196–212.

Favre, M. R., La Mendola, D., Meystre, J. et al. (2015). Predictable enriched environment prevents development of hyper-emotionality in the VPA rat model of autism. *Frontiers in Neuroscience, 9,* 127.

Feinberg, M. E., Soimeyer, A. R., & McHale, S. M. (2012). The third rail of family systems: Sibling relationships, mental and behavioral health, and preventive intervention in childhood and adolescence. *Clinical Child and Family Psychology Review, 15,* 43–57.

Fernald, R. D., & Maruska, K. P. (2012). Social information changes the brain. *PNAS*, *109*(Suppl. 2), 17194–17199.

Fiadzo, E. (2004). *Estimating the Determinants of Housing Quality: The Case of Ghana.* www.jchs.harvard.edu/sites/jchs.harvard.edu/files/w04-6.pdf

Fischer, K. W. (1980). A theory of cognitive development: The control and construction of hierarchies of skill. *Psychological Review*, *87*, 477–531.

Fish, A., Li, X., McCarrick, K. et al. (2008). Early childhood computer experience and cognitive among urban, low-income preschoolers. *Journal of Educational Computing Research*, *38*, 97–113.

Fontanella, C A., Hiance-Steelesmith, D. L., Phillips, G. S. et al. (2015). Widening rural-urban disparities in youth suicides United States, 1996–2010. *JAMA Pediatrics*, *169*, 466–473.

Folke, C. (2006). Resilience: The emergence of a perspective for social-ecological systems analysis. *Global Environmental Change*, *16*, 253–267.

Food and Agriculture Organization of the United Nations. (2017). *Child Labor in Agriculture.* www.fao.org/childlabouragriculture/en/

Ford, D. H., & Lerner, R. M. (1992). *Developmental Systems Theory: An Integrative Approach.* Newbury Park, CA: Sage.

Fox, S. E., Levitt, P., & Nelson, C. A. (2010). How the timing and quality of early experiences influence the development of brain architecture. *Child Development*, *81*, 28–40.

Fraillon, J., Ainley, J., Schulz, W. et al. (2014). The influence of students' personal and home background on computer and information literacy. In J. Fraillon, J. Ainley, W. Schulz, T. Friedman, & E. Bebhardt (Eds.), *Preparing for Life in a Digital Age* (pp. 101–124). Cham: Springer.

Frank, R. G., & Meara, E. (2009). The effect of maternal depression and substance abuse on child human capital development. National Bureau of Economic Research, Working Paper 15314. www.nber.org/papers/w15314

Frith, U., & Frith, C. (2001). The biological basis of social interaction. *Current Directions in Psychological Science*, *10*, 151–155.

Fuentes, R., Pfutze, R., & Seck, P. (2006). Does access to water and sanitation affect child survival: A five country analysis. Occasional Paper 2006/4. Human Development Reports, United Nations Development Programme. http://hdr.undp.org/en/content/does-access-water-and-sanitation-affect-child-survival

Funk, L. M, Allan, D. E., & Chappell, N. L. (2007). Testing the relationship between involvement and perceived neighborhood safety. *Environment and Behavior*, *39*, 332–351.

Geens, N., & Vandenbroeck, M. (2012). The (ab)sense of a concept of social support in parenting research: A social work perspective. *Child and Family Social Work*, *19*, 491–500.

Gershoff, E. T. (2013). Spanking and child development: We know enough to stop hitting our children. *Child Development Perspectives*, *7*, 133–137.

Gerwitz, A., Forgatch, M., & Wieling, E. (2008). Parenting practices as potential mechanisms for child adjustment following mass trauma. *Journal of Marital and Family Therapy*, *34*, 177–192.

Gielen, A., Shields, W., McDonald, E. et al. (2012). Home safety and low-income housing quality. *Pediatrics*, *130*, 1053–1059.

Gilkerson J., Richards, J., Warren, S. et al. (2018). Language experience in the second year of life and language outcomes in late childhood. *Pediatrics*, *142*, 74276.

Goldstein, T. R., & Lerner, M. D. (2018). Dramatic pretend play games uniquely improve emotional control in young children. *Developmental Science*, *21*, e12603.

Gonzales, N. A., Coxe, S., Roosa, M. W. et al. (2011). Mexican-American adolescent's mental health. *American Journal of Community Psychology*, *47*, 98–113.

Goux, D., & Maurin, E. (2003). The effect of overcrowded housing on children's performance at school. *Journal of Public Economics*, *89*, 797–819.

Greenberg, M. T., Lengua, L. J., Coie, J. D. et al. (1999). Predicting developmental outcomes at school entry using a multiple-risk model: Four American communities. *Developmental Psychology*, *35*, 403–417.

Gruebner, O., Rapp, M. A., Adli, M. et al. (2017). Cities and mental health. *Deutsches Arzteblatt International*, *114*, 121–127.

Grummer-Strawn, L. M., Li, R., Perrine, C. G. et al. (2014). Infant feeding and long-term outcomes: Results from the Year 6 follow-up of children in the Infant Feeding Practices Study II. *Pediatrics*, *134* (Suppl. 1), 81–83.

Grusec, J. E. (2011). Socialization processes in the family: Social and emotional development. *Annual Review of Psychology*, *62*, 243–269.

Grusec, J. E., & Davidov, M. (2010). Integrating different perspectives on socialization theory and research: A domain-specific approach. *Child Development*, *81*, 687–709.

Gunning, M., Conroy, S., Valoriani, V. et al. (2004). Measurement of mother-infant interactions and the home environment in a European setting: Preliminary results from a cross-cultural study. *British Journal of Psychiatry*, *184*(Suppl. 46), E38–E44.

Guralnick, M. J., Connor, R. T., & Johnson, L. C. (2009). Home-based peer social networks of young children with Down syndrome: A developmental perspective. *American Journal of Intellectual and Developmental Disabilities*, 114, 340–365.

Hajizadeh, S., Tehrani, F. R., Simbar, J. et al. (2016), Factors influencing the use of prenatal care. *Journal of Midwifery and Reproductive Health*, *4*, 544–557.

Hamadani, J. D., Tofail, F., Huda, S. N. et al. (2014). Cognitive deficit and poverty in the first 5 years of childhood in Bangladesh. *Pediatrics, 134*, e1001–e1008.

Hameed, M. A., & Lewis, A. J. (2016). Offspring of parents with schizophrenia: A systematic review of developmental features across childhood. *Harvard Review of Psychiatry, 24*, 104–117.

Hammond, S. I., Kulrich, M., Carpendale, J. I. et al. (2012). The effects of parental scaffolding on preschoolers' executive function. *Developmental Psychology, 48*, 271–281.

Han, C. S., Masse, L. C., Wilson, A. et al. (2018). State of play: Methodologies for investigating children's outdoor play and independent mobility. *Children, Youth, and Environments, 28*, 194–231.

Hancock, K. J., Cunningham, N. K., Lawrence, D. et al. (2015). Playgroup participation and social support outcomes for mothers of young children: A longitudinal cohort study. *PLoS ONE, 10*(7), e0133007.

Hand, K. L., Freeman, C., Seddon, P. J. et al. (2018). Restricted home ranges reduce children's opportunities to connect to nature: Demographic, environmental and parental influences. *Landscape and Urban Planning, 172*, 69–77.

Hardy, L., Baur, L., Garnett, S. et al. (2006). Family and home correlates of television viewing in 12–13-year old adolescents: The Nepean study. *International Journal of Behavioral Nutrition and Physical Activity, 3*, 24.

Harmon-Jones, E., Gable, P. A., & Peterson, C. K. (2010). The role of asymmetric frontal cortical activity in emotion-related phenomena: A review and update. *Biological Psychology, 84*, 451–462.

Hart, B., & Risley, T. (1995). *Meaningful Differences in the Everyday Experience of Young American Children*. Baltimore: Brookes.

Hart, C. H., DeWolf, D. M., Wozniak, P. et al. (1992). Maternal and paternal disciplinary styles: Relations with preschoolers' playground behavioral orientations and peer status. *Child Development, 63*, 879–892.

Hartig, T., Mitchell, R., de Vries, S. et al. (2014). Nature and health. *Annual Review of Public Health, 35*, 207–228.

Hartwell-Rocker, M. (2018). Children who are home alone. *PsycCentral*, October. https://psychcentral.com/lib/children-who-are-home-alone/

Hauenstein, E. J. (2008). Building the rural mental health system: From de facto system to quality care. *Annual Review of Nursing Research, 26*, 143–173.

Hayward, R. A., Depanfilis, D., & Woodruff, K. (2010). Parental methamphetamine use and implications for child welfare intervention: A review of the literature. *Journal of Public Child Welfare, 4*, 25–60.

Health and Places Initiative. (2014). *Geographic Healthcare Access and Place. A Research Brief*. Version 1.0. http://research.gsd.harvard.edu/hapi/

Healthy People 2020. (2019). *Access to Health Services*, December. www .healthypeople.gov/2020/topics-objectives/topic/Access-to-Health-Services

Heft, H. (1993). A methodological note on overestimates of reaching distance: Distinguishing between perceptual and analytical judgments. *Ecological Psychology, 5*, 255–271.

Heft, H. (2018). Places: Widening the scope of an ecological approach to perception-action with an emphasis on child development. *Ecological Psychology, 30*, 99–123.

Henly, J. R., & Adams, G. (2018). *Increasing Access to Quality Child Care for Four Priority Populations*. Research Report, Urban Institute, October. www .urban.org/sites/default/files/publication/99150/increasing_access_to_quali ty_child_care_for_four_priority_populations_report_3.pdf

Henning-Smith, C., & Kozhimannil, K. B. (2016). Availability of child care in rural communities: Implications for workforce recruitment and retention. *Journal of Community Health, 41*, 488–493.

Hetherington, E. M., & Stanley-Hagan, M. (1999). The adjustment of children with divorced parents: A risk and resiliency perspective. *Journal of Child Psychology and Psychiatry, 40*, 129–140.

Hoffman, C., Crnic, K., & Baker, J. (2006). Maternal depression and parenting: Implications for children's emergent emotional regulation and behavioral functioning. *Parenting: Science and Practice, 6*, 271–295.

Holland, J. H. (1992). Complex adaptive systems. *Daedalus, 121*, 17–30.

Hollingsworth, S., Mansaray, A., & Allen, A. (2011). Parents' perspectives on technology and children's learning in the home: Social class and the role of habitus. *Journal of Computer Assisted Learning, 27*, 347–360.

Horn, S. R., Miller-Graff, L. E., Galano, M. M. et al. (2017). Posttraumatic stress disorder in children exposed to intimate partner violence: The clinical picture of physiological arousal symptoms. *Child Care & Practice, 23*, 90–103.

Hoover-Dempsey, K. V. Battiato, A. C., Walker, J. M. et al. (2001). Parental involvement in homework. *Educational Psychologist, 36*, 195–209.

Horvat, E., Weininger, E., & Lareau, A. (2003). From social ties to social capital: Class differences in the relations between schools and parent networks. *American Educational Research Journal, 40*, 319–351.

Housing Assistance Council. (2012). *Taking Stock, Rural People, Poverty, and Housing in the 21st Century*. Report. www.ruralhome.org/storage/docu ments/ts2010/ts_full_report.pdf

Howard, L. M., Kumar, R., & Thornicroft, G. (2001). Psychosocial characteristics and needs of mothers with psychotic disorders. *British Journal of Psychiatry, 178*, 427–432.

Hsin, A., & Felfe, C. (2014). When does time matter? Maternal employment children's time with parents and child development. *Demography, 51*, 1867–1894.

Hunt, S. M. (1990). Emotional distress and bad housing. *Health and Hygiene, 11*, 72–79.

Hurley, K. M., Black, M. M., Merry, B. C. et al. (2015). Maternal mental health and infant dietary patterns in a statewide sample of Maryland WIC participants. *Maternal and Child Nutrition, 11*, 229–239.

Hurwitz, L. B. (2019). Getting ready to learn media: A meta-analytic review of effects on literacy. *Child Development, 90*, 1754–1771.

Hutton, J. S., Dudley, J., Horowitz-Kraus, T. et al. (2020). Associations between screen-based media use and brain white matter integrity in preschool-aged children. *JAMA Pediatrics, 174*, e193869.

Hygge, S., Evans, G. W., & Bullinger, M. (2002). A prospective study of some effects of aircraft noise on cognitive performance in schoolchildren. *Psychological Science, 13*, 469–474.

Iaupuni, S. M., Donato, K., Thompson-Colon, T. et al. (2005). Counting on kin: Social networks, social support, and child health status. *Social Forces, 83*, 1137–1164.

Iezzoni, L. I., Killeen, M. B., & O'Day, B. L. (2006). Rural residents with disabilities confront substantial barriers to obtaining primary care. *Health Services Research, 41*, 1258–1275.

International Organization of Migration. (2014). Migration and families. Background Paper, International Dialogue on Migration (IDM) 2014 Workshop, October 7–8. www.iom.int/files/live/sites/iom/files/What-We-Do/idm/workshops/Migrants-and-Families-2014/IDM-October-2014-Migration-and-Families-Background-paper.pdf

Islam, M. Z., Moore, R., & Cosco, N. (2016). Child-friendly, active, healthy neighborhoods: Physical characteristics and children's time outdoors. *Environment and Behavior, 48*, 711–736.

Jaffee, J., Beebe, B., Feldstein, F. et al. (2001). Rhythms of dialogue in infancy: Coordinated timing in development. *Monographs of the Society for Research in Child Development, 66*(2).

Jaffee, S., Hanscombe, B., Haworth, C. et al. (2012). Chaotic homes and children's disruptive behavior: A longitudinal cross-lagged twin study. *Psychological Science, 23*, 643–650.

Jago, R., Stamatakis, E., Gama, A. et al. (2012). Parent and child screen-viewing time and home media environment. *American Journal of Preventive Medicine, 43*, 150–158.

Jaishankar, M., Tseten, T., Anbalagan, N. et al. (2014). Toxicity, mechanism and health effects of some heavy metals. *Interdisciplinary Toxicology, 7*, 60–72.

James, C., Davis, K., Charmaraman, L. et al. (2017). Digital life and youth well-being, social connectedness, empathy, and narcissism. *Pediatrics, 140*, S71.

Janevic, T., Petrivoc, O., Bjelic, I. et al. (2010). Risk factors for childhood malnutrition in Roma settlements in Serbia. *BMC Public Health, 10*, 509.

Jaskiewicz, M., & Wiwatowska, E. (2018). Perceived neighborhood disorder and quality of life: The role of human place bond, social interactions, and out-group blaming. *Journal of Environmental Psychology, 58*, 31–41.

Jelleyman, T., & Spencer, N. (2008). Residential mobility in childhood and health outcomes: A systematic review. *Journal of Epidemiology and Community Health, 62*, 584–592.

Johnson, G. (2010). Internet use and child development: Validation of the ecological techno-subsystem. *Educational Technology and Society, 13*, 176–185.

Johnson, J. L., & Leff, M. (1999). Children of substance abusers Overview of research findings. *Pediatrics, 103*, 1085–1099

Johnson, S. B., Riis, J. L., & Noble, K. G. (2016). Poverty and the developing brain. *Pediatrics, 137*, e20153075.

Jones, D. J., Forehand, R., Brody, G. et al. (2002). Psychosocial adjustment of African American children in single mother families: A test of three risk models. *Journal of Marriage and Family, 64*, 105–115.

Jones, D. J., Forehand, R., O'Connell, C. et al. (2005). Mothers' perceptions of neighborhood violence and mother-reported monitoring of African American children: An examination of the moderating role of perceived support. *Behavior Therapy, 36*, 25–34.

Kaczynski, A., & Henderson, K. (2007). Environmental correlates of physical activity: A review of evidence about parks and recreation. *Leisure Science, 29*, 315–354.

Kagan, J. (2003). Biology, context, and developmental inquiry. *Annual Review of Psychology, 54*, 1–23.

Kahn, R. S., Brandt, D., & Whitaker, R. C. (2004). Combined effects of mothers and fathers' mental health symptoms on children's behavioral and emotional well-being. *Archives of Pediatrics and Adolescent Medicine, 158*, 721–728.

Kant, A. K., & Graubard, B. I. (2012). Race-ethnic, family income, and education differentials in nutritional and lipid biomarkers in US children and adolescents: NHANES 2003–2006. *American Journal of Clinical Nutrition, 96*, 601–612.

Karstad, S. B., Kvello, O., Wichstrom, L. et al. (2014). What do parents know about their children's comprehension of emotions? Accuracy of parental estimates in a community sample of pre-schoolers. *Child: Care Health and Development, 40*, 346–353.

Katz, V. S., Gonzalez, C., & Clark, K. (2017). Digital inequality and developmental trajectories of low-income, immigrant, and minority children. *Pediatrics, 140*, e20161758.

Keller, J., Yovsi, R., Borke, J. et al. (2004). Developmental consequences of early parenting experiences: Self-recognition and self-regulation in three cultural communities. *Child Development, 75*, 1745–1760.

Kellner, C. J., Brawn, J. D., & Karr J. R. (1992). What is habitat suitability and how should it be measured? In D. R. McCullough & R. H. Barrett (Eds.), *Wildlife 2001: Populations* (pp. 476–488). Dordrecht: Springer.

Kiernan, K., & Huerta, M. C. (2008). Economic deprivation, maternal depression, parenting and children's cognitive and emotional development in early childhood. *The British Journal of Sociology, 59*, 783–806.

Kirkorian, H., Wartella, E., & Anderson, D. (2008). Media and young children's learning. *The Future of Children, 18*, 39–61.

Koblinsky, S. A., Kuvalanka, K. A., & Randolph, S. M. (2006). Social skills and behavior problems of urban, African American preschoolers: Role of parenting practices, family conflict, and maternal depression. *American Journal of Orthopsychiatry, 76*, 554–563.

Kohen, D., Leventhal, T., Dahinten, V. S. et al. (2008). Neighborhood disadvantage: Pathways of effect for young children. *Child Development, 79*, 156–169.

Kohl, P. L., Jonson-Reid, M, & Drake, B. (2011). Maternal mental illness and the safety and stability of maltreated children. *Child Abuse and Neglect, 35*, 309–318.

Koolick, J., Galano, M., Grogan-Kaylor, A. et al. (2016). PTSD symptoms in young children exposed to intimate partner violence in four ethno-racial groups. *Journal of Child & Adolescent Trauma, 9*, 97–107.

Korpela, K. M., Kytta, M., & Hartig, T. (2002). Children's favorite places: Restorative experience, self-regulation and children's place preferences. *Journal of Environmental Psychology, 22*, 387–398.

Kosic, A., Kruglanski, A. W., Pierro, A. et al. (2008). The social cognition of immigrants' acculturation: Effects of the need for closure and the reference group at entry. *Journal of Personality & Social Psychology, 86*, 796–813.

Koury, A., & Vortruba-Drzal, E. (2014). School readiness of children from immigrant families: Contribution of region of origin, home, and childcare. *Journal of Educational Psychology, 106*, 268–288.

Krishnakumar, A., & Buehler, C. (2000). Interparental conflict and parenting behaviors: A meta-analytic review. *Family Relations, 49*, 25–44.

Kundakovic, M., & Champagne, F. A. (2014). Early-life experience, epigenetics, and the developing brain. *Neuropsychopharmacology, 40*, 141–153.

Kyatta, M. (2002). The affordances of children's environments in the context of cities, small towns, suburbs and rural villages in Finland and Belarus. *Journal of Environmental Psychology, 22*, 109–123.

Lai, A., & Maclean, R. (2011). Children on the move: The impact of involuntary and voluntary migration on the lives of children. *Global Studies of Childhood, 1*, 87–91.

Lamela, D., & Figueiredo, B. (2016). Coparenting after marital dissolution and children's mental health: A systematic review. *Jornal de Pediatria, 92*, 331–342.

Lander, L., Howsare, J., & Byrne, M. (2013). The impact of substance abuse disorders on families and children: From theory to practice. *Social Work and Public Health, 28*, 194–205

Lansdale, N. S., Thomas, K. J., & Van Hook J. (2011). The living arrangements of immigrant children. *The Future of Children, 21*, 43–70.

Lander, L., Howsare, J., & Byrne, M. (2013). The impact of substance abuse disorders on families and children: From theory to practice. *Social Work and Public Health, 28*, 194–205.

Lannert, B. K., Garcia, A. M., Smagur, K. E. et al. (2014). Relational trauma in the context of intimate partner violence. *Child Abuse and Neglect, 38*, 1966–1975.

Lansford, J. E. (2009). Parental divorce and children's adjustment. *Perspectives on Psychological Science, 4*, 140–152.

Laursen, L. L., Madsen, K. B., Obel, C. et al. (2019). Family dissolution and children's social well-being at school: A historic cohort study. *BMC Pediatrics, 19*, 449

Larzelere, R. E. (2000). Child outcomes of nonabusive and customary physical punishment by parents: An updated literature review. *Clinical Child & Family Psychology Review, 3*, 199–221.

Lauricella, A., Pempek, T., Barr, R. et al. (2010). Contingent computer interactions for young children's object retrieval success. *Journal of Applied Developmental Psychology, 31*, 362–369.

Lederbogen, F., Kirsch, P., Haddad, L. et al. (2011). City living and urban upbringing affect neural social stress processing in humans. *Nature, 472*, 498–501.

Lee, D., & McLanahan, S. (2015). Family structure transitions and child development: Instability, selection, and population heterogeneity. *American Sociological Review, 80*, 238–263.

Lee, H., & Williams, R. A. (2013). Effects of parental alcoholism, sense of belonging, and resilience on depressive symptoms: A path model. *Substance Use and Misuse, 48*, 265–273.

LeFevre, J-A., Skwarchuk, S-L., Smith-Chant, B. et al. (2010). Pathways to mathematics: Longitudinal predictors of performance. *Child Development, 81,* 1753–1767.

Lehrl, S., Ebert, S., Sabine Blaurock, S. et al. (2019). Long-term and domain-specific relations between the early years home learning environment and students' academic outcomes in secondary school. *School Effectiveness and School Improvement.* https://doi.org/10.1080/09243453 .2019.1618346

Leibham, M. E., Alexander, J. M., Johnson, K. E. et al. (2005). Parenting behaviors associated with the maintenance of preschoolers' interests: A prospective longitudinal study. *Applied Developmental Psychology, 26,* 397–414.

Leonard, K. E., & Eiden, R. D. (2007). Marital and family processes in the context of alcohol use and alcohol disorders. *Annual Review of Clinical Psychology, 3,* 285–310.

Leonhard, M. J., Wright, D. A., Fu, R. et al. (2015). Urban/rural disparities in Oregon pediatric traumatic brain injury. *Injury Epidemiology, 2,* 32.

Letourneau, N., Salmani, M., & Duffett-Leger, L. (2010). Maternal depressive symptoms and parenting of children from birth to 12 years. *Western Journal of Nursing Research, 32,* 662–685.

Leventhal, T., & Brooks-Gunn, J. (2000). The neighborhoods they live in: The effects of neighborhood residence on child and adolescent outcomes. *Psychological Bulletin, 126,* 309–337.

Lewicka, M. (2011). Place attachment: How far have we come in the last 40 years? *Journal of Environmental Psychology, 31,* 207–230.

Lewis, M. D. (2000). The promise of dynamic systems approaches for an integrated account of human development. *Child Development, 71,* 36–43.

Lieberman, D., Fisk, M., & Biely, E. (2009). Digital games for young children ages three to six: From research to design. *Computers in the Schools, 26,* 299–313.

Lien, H.-M., Wu, W.-C., & Lin, C.-C. (2008). New evidence on the link between housing environment and children's educational attainments. *Journal of Urban Economics, 64,* 408–421.

Lipari, R. N., & Van Horn, S. L. (2017). Children Living with Parents Who Have a Substance Use Disorder. Center for Behavioral Health Statistics and Quality (CBHSQ) Report, CBHSQ and Substance Abuse and Mental Health Services Administration, Rockville, MD, August 24. www.samhsa.gov/data/ sites/default/files/report_3223/ShortReport-3223.html

Livingstone, S., & Helsper, E. (2008). Parental mediation and children's Internet use. *Journal of Broadcasting & Electronic Media, 52,* 581–599.

Livingstone, S., Mascheroni, G., Dreier, M. et al. (2015). *How Parents of Young Children Manage Digital Devices at Home: The Role of Income, Education and Parental Style*. London: EU Kids Online.

Lovejoy, M. C., Graczyk, P. A., O'Hare, E., & Neuman, G. (2000). Maternal depression and parenting behavior: A meta-analytic review. *Clinical Psychology Review, 20*, 561–592.

Lowe, S., Erickson, S., MacLean, P. et al. (2013). Association of maternal scaffolding to maternal education and cognition in toddlers both preterm and full term. *Acta Paediatrica, 102*, 72–77.

Luciano, A., Nicholson, J., & Meara, E. (2014). The economic status of parents with serious mental illness in the United States. *Psychiatric Rehabilitation Journal, 37*, 242–250.

MacKinnon, C., Brody, G., & Stoneman, Z. (1982). The effects of divorce and maternal employment on the home environments of preschool children. *Child Development, 53*, 1392–1399.

Mahoney, J. L., Harris, A. L., & Eccles, J. S. (2006). Organized activity participation, positive youth development, and the over-scheduling hypothesis. *Society for Research in Child Development: Social Policy Report, 20*, 1–30.

Manly, J. T., Lynch, M., Oshri, A. et al. (2013). The impact of neglect on initial adaptation to school. *Child Maltreatment, 18*, 155–170.

Manolitsis, R., Georgiou, G. K., & Tziraki, N. (2013). Examining the effects of home literacy and numeracy environment on early reading and math acquisition. *Early Childhood Research Quarterly, 28*, 692–703.

Marcs, M., & Woodard, E. (2005). Positive effects of television on children's social interactions: A meta-analysis. *Media Psychology, 7*, 301–322.

Martin, A., Razza, R., & Brooks-Gunn, J. (2012). Specifying links between household chaos and preschool children's development. *Early Child Development and Care, 182*, 1247–1263.

Martin, K. S., Rogers, B. L, Cook, J. T. et al. (2004). Social capital is associated with decreased risk of hunger. *Social Science and Medicine, 58*, 2645–2654.

Mattejat, F., & Remschmidt, H. (2008). The children of mentally ill parents. *Deutsches Arzteblatt International, 105*, 413–418.

Mayberry, L. S., Shinn, M., Benton, J. G. et al. (2014). Families experiencing housing instability: The effects of housing programs on family routines and rituals. *American Journal of Orthopsychiatry, 84*, 95–109.

Maynard, T., & Waters, J. (2007). Learning in the outdoor environment: A missed opportunity? *Early Years, 27*, 255–265.

McClure, E. R., Chentsova-Dutton, Y. E., Holochwost, S. J. et al. (2018). Look at that! Video chat and joint visual attention development among babies and toddlers. *Child Development, 89*, 27–36.

McConnell, D., Breitkreuz, R., & Savage A. (2011). From financial hardship to child difficulties: Main and moderating effects of perceived social support. *Child: Care, Health and Development, 37,* 679–691.

McCormack, L. A., & Meendering, J. (2016). Diet and physical activity in rural vs urban children and adolescents in the United States: A narrative review. *Journal of the Academy of Nutrition and Dietetics, 116,* 467–480.

McCracken, J. P., Smith, K. R., Diaz, A. et al. (2007). Chimney stove intervention to reduce long-term wood smoke exposure lowers blood pressure among Guatemalan women. *Environmental Health Perspectives, 115,* 996–1001.

McDaniel, B. T. (2019). Parent distraction with phones, reasons for use, and impacts on parenting and child outcomes: A review of emerging research. *Human Behavior and Emerging Technology, 1,* 72–80.

McDonnell, J. R. (2007). Neighborhood characteristics, parenting, and children's safety. *Social Indicators Research, 83,* 177–199.

McDonough, C., Song, L., Hirsh Pasek, K. et al. (2011). An image is worth a thousand words: Why nouns tend to dominate verbs in early word learning. *Developmental Science, 14,* 181–189.

McEniry, M. (2013). Early life conditions and older adult health in low- and middle-income countries: A review. *Journal on the Developmental Origins of Health and Disease, 4,* 10–29.

McEwen, B. S., & Gianaros, P. J. (2010). Central role of the brain in stress and adaptation: Links to socioeconomic status, health, and disease. *Annals of the New York Academy of Sciences, 1186,* 190–222.

McHale, S. M, Dotterer, A., & Kim, J-Y. (2009). An ecological perspective on the media and youth development. *American Behavioral Scientist, 52,* 1186–1203.

McLoyd, V. C., Toyokawa, T., & Kaplan, R. (2008). Work demands, work family conflict, and child adjustment in African American families: The mediating role of family routines. *Journal of Family Issues, 29,* 1247–1267.

McMichael, C. (2019). Water, sanitation, and hygiene (WASH) in schools in low-income countries: A review of evidence of impact. *International Journal of Environmental Research and Public Health, 16,* 359.

Meit, M., Knudson, A., Gilbert, T. et al. (2014). *The 2014 Update of the Rural-Urban Chartbook,* October. Rural Health Reform Policy Research Center. https://ruralhealth.und.edu/projects/health-reform-policy-research-center/pdf/2014-rural-urban-chartbook-update.pdf

Melhuish, E., Phan, M., Sylva, K. et al. (2008). The effects of the home learning environment and preschool center experience upon literacy and numeracy development in early primary school. *Journal of Social Issues, 64,* 95–114.

Meltzer, A., Muir, K., & Craig, L. (2018). The role of trusted adults in young people's social and economic lives. *Youth and Society, 50,* 575–592.

Mesch, G. (2006). Family relations and the internet: Exploring a family boundaries approach. *Journal of Family Communication, 6,* 119–138.

Meyers, S. R., Branas, C. C., French, B. C. et al. (2013). Safety in numbers: Are major cities the safest places in the United States? *Annals of Emergency Medicine, 62,* 408–418.

Middleton, N., Gunnell, D., Frankel, S. et al. (2003). Urban-rural differences in suicide trends in young adults: England and Wales, 1981–1998. *Social Science and Medicine, 57,* 1183–1194.

Miles, R. (2008). Neighborhood disorder, perceived safety, and readiness to encourage use of local playgrounds. *American Journal of Preventive Medicine, 34,* 275–281.

Miller, A., Hess, J. M., Bybee, D. et al. (2018). Understanding the mental health consequences of family separation for refugees: Implications for policy and practice. *American Journal of Orthopsychiatry, 88,* 26–37.

Miller, G. E., & Chen, E. (2013). The biological residue of childhood poverty. *Child Development Perspectives, 2,* 67–73.

Miller, P., & Vortruba-Drzal, E. (2013). Early academic skills and childhood experiences across the urban-rural continuum. *Early Childhood Research Quarterly, 28,* 234–248.

Minh, A., Muhajarine, N., Janus, M. et al. (2017). A review of neighborhood effects and early child development: How, where, and for whom, do neighborhoods matter? *Health and Place, 46,* 155–174.

Misra, S., Cheng, L., Genevie, J. et al. (2014). The iPhone effect: The quality of in-person social interactions in the presence of mobile device. *Environment and Behavior, 48,* 1–24.

Mistry, R. S., Lowe, E. D., Benner, A. D. et al. (2008). Expanding the family economic stress model: Insights from a mixed-methods approach. *Journal of Marriage and Family, 70,* 196–209.

Mock, N. B., Sellers, T. A., Abdoh, A. A. et al. (1993). Socio-economic, environmental, demographic and behavioral factors associated with occurrence of diarrhea in young children in the Republic of Congo. *Social Science and Medicine, 36,* 807–816.

Morgan, P. (2010). Towards a developmental theory of place attachment. *Journal of Environmental Psychology, 30,* 11–22.

Morenikeji, W., Umaru, E., Pai, H. et al. (2017). Spatial analysis of housing quality in Nigeria. *International Journal of Sustainable Built Environment, 6,* 309–316.

Morrissey, T. (2009). Multiple child-care arrangements and young children's behavioral outcomes. *Child Development, 80*, 59–76.

Morrongiello, B., Kane, A. K., & Zdzieborski, D. (2011). "I think he is in his room playing a video game": Parental supervision of young elementary-school children at home. *Journal of Pediatric Psychology, 36*, 708–717.

Morrongiello, B. A., Klemencic, N., & Corbett, M. (2008). Interactions between child behavior patterns and parent supervision: Implications for children's risk of injury. *Child Development, 79*, 627–638.

Morrongiello, B. A., MacIsaac, T., & Klemencic, N. (2007). Older siblings as supervisors: Does this influence young children's risk of unintentional injury? *Social Science and Medicine, 64*, 807–817.

Mullan, K., & Chatzitheochari, S. (2019). Changing times together? A time-diary analysis of family time in the digital age in the United Kingdom. *Journal of Marriage and Family, 81*, 795–811.

Muniz, E., Silver, E., & Stein, R. (2014). Family routines and social-emotional school readiness among preschool-age children. *Journal of Developmental and Behavioral Pediatrics, 35*, 93–99.

Murphey, E., Bandy, T., & Moore, K. A. (2012). *Frequent Residential Mobility and Young Children's Well-Being*. Child Trends Research Brief No. 2012–02, January. www.childtrends.org/publications/frequent-residential-mobility-and-young-childrens-well-being

Nairn, K., Panelli, R., & McCormack, J. (2003). Destabilizing dualisms, Young people's experiences of rural and urban environments. *Childhood, 10*, 9–42.

Nandy, S., & Gordon, D. (2009). Children living in squalor: Shelter, water and sanitation deprivations in developing countries. *Children, Youth and Environments, 19*, 202–229.

Nathanson, A., & Cantor, J. (2000). Reducing the aggression-promoting effect of violent cartoons by increasing children's fictional involvement with the victim: A study of active mediation. *Journal of Broadcasting and Electronic Media, 44*, 125–144.

National Research Council & Institute of Medicine. (2009). *Depression in Parents, Parenting, and Children: Opportunities to Improve Identification, Treatment, and Prevention*. Washington, DC: The National Academies Press.

Nestadt, P. S., Triplett, P., Fowler, D. R. et al. (2017). Urban-rural differences in the state of Maryland: The role of firearms. *American Journal of Public Health, 107*, 1548–1553.

Neufeld, J. E., Rasmussen, H. N., Lopez, S. J. et al. (2006). The engagement model of person-environment interaction. *The Counseling Psychologist, 34*, 245–259.

NICHD Early Child Care Research Network. (2000). Factors associated with father's caregiving activities and sensitivity with young children. *Journal of Family Psychology, 14*, 200–219.

Nikken P., & Schols, M. (2015). How and why parents guide the media use of young children. *Journal of Child and Family Studies, 24*, 3432–3435.

Noll, R. B., Zuker, R. A., Fitzgerald, H. E. et al. (1992). Cognitive and motor achievement of sons of alcoholic fathers and controls: The early childhood years. *Developmental Psychology, 28*, 665–675.

Norholt, H. (2020). Revisiting the roots of attachment: A review of the biological and psychological effects of maternal skin-to-skin contact and carrying of full-term infants. *Infant Behavior & Development, 60*, e101441.

NPD Group. (2009). *Kids' Use of Consumer Electronics Devices Such as Cell Phones, Personal Computers, and Video Game Platforms Continue to Rise*, NPD Group Press Release, June 9. www.npd.com/ press/releases/ press_090609a.html

Nriagu, J., Martin, J., Smith, P. et al. (2012). Residential hazards, high asthma prevalence and multimorbidity among children in Saginaw, Michigan. *Science of the Total Environment, 416*, 53–61.

Oakes, M. (2009). The effect of media on children: A methodological assessment from a social epidemiologist. *American Behavioral Scientist, 52*, 1136–1151.

Ohrstrom, E., Hadzibajramovic, E., Holmes, M. et al. (2006). Effects of road traffic noise on sleep: Studies on children and adults. *Journal of Environmental Psychology, 26*, 116–126.

O'Keefe, G. S., Clarke-Pearson, K., & Council on Communications and Media. (2011). The impact of social media on children, adolescents, and families. *Pediatrics, 127*, 800–804.

Olsen, S. F., Marshall, E. S., Mandleco, B. L. et al. (1999). Support, communication, and hardiness in families with children with disabilities. *Journal of Family Nursing, 5*, 275–291.

O'Neil, R., Parke, R. D., & McDowell, D. J. (2001). Objective and subjective features of children's neighborhoods: Relations to parental regulatory strategies and children's social competence. *Applied Developmental Psychology, 22*, 135–155.

Ostrosky, M. & Meadan, H. (2010). Helping children play and learn together. *Young Children, 65*, 104–110.

Oyserman, D., Mowbray, C. T., Meares, P. A. et al. (2000). Parenting among mothers with a serious mental illness. *American Journal of Orthopsychiatry, 70*, 296–315.

Palfreyman, Z., Haycraft, E., & Meyer C. (2014). Development of the Parental Modeling of Eating Behaviours Scale (PARM): Links with food intake among children and their mothers. *Maternal and Child Nutrition*, *10*, 619–629.

Parcel, T. L., & Bixby, M. S. (2016). The ties that bind: Social capital, families, and children's well-being. *Child Development Perspectives*, *10*, 87–92.

Paulus, M. P., Squeglia, L. M., Bagot, K. et al. (2019). Screen media activity and brain structure in youth: Evidence for diverse structural correlation networks from the ABCD study. *Neuroimage*, *185*, 140–153.

Pea, R. D. (2004). The social and technological dimensions of scaffolding and related theoretical concepts for learning, education, and human activity. *The Journal of Learning Sciences*, *13*, 423–451.

Pearce, A., Li, L., Abbas, J. et al. (2012). Childcare use and inequalities in breastfeeding: Findings from the UK Millennium Cohort Study. *Archives of Diseases in Childhood*, *97*, 39–42.

Pearson, N., Biddle, S., & Gorely, T. (2009). Family correlates of fruit and vegetable consumption in children and adolescents: a systematic review. *Public Health and Nutrition*, *12*, 267–283.

Perrin, A. (2019). Digital gap between rural and nonrural America persists. *Fact Tank, News in the Numbers*, May 31. Pew Research Center. Available at: https://www.pewresearch.org/fact-tank/2019/05/31/digital-gap-between-rural-and-nonrural-america-persists/.

Perrin, E. C., Leslie, L. K., & Boat, T. (2016). Parenting as primary prevention. *JAMA Pediatrics*, *170*, 637–638.

Perry, N. B., Dollar, J. M., Calkins, S. D. et al. (2018). Childhood self-regulation as mechanism through which early overcontrolling parenting is associated with adjustment in adolescence. *Developmental Psychology*, *54*, 1542–1554.

Petrides, K. V., Sangareau, Y., Furnham, A. et al. (2006). Trait emotional intelligence and children's peer relations at school. *Social Development*, *3*, 537–547.

Petrill, S. A., Pike, A., Price, T. et al. (2004). Chaos in the home and socioeconomic status are associated with cognitive development in early childhood: Environmental mediators identified in a genetic design. *Intelligence*, *32*, 445–460.

Pettit, G. S., Dodge, K. A., & Brown, M. M. (1988). Early family experience, social problem-solving patterns, and children's social competence. *Child Development*, *59*, 107–120.

Pew Research Center. (2013). *Parents, Children, Libraries, and Reading*, Report, May 1. http://libraries.pewinternet.org/2013/05/01/parents-children-libraries-and-reading/

Pew Research Center. (2015). *Parenting in America*, Report, December 17. www.pewsocialtrends.org/2015/12/17/parenting-in-america/

Pew Research Center. (2016). *Parents, Teens, and Digital Monitoring*, January 7. www.pewresearch.org/internet/2016/01/07/parents-teens-and-digital-monitoring/

Pew Research Center. (2018). *What Unites and Divides Urban, Suburban, and Rural Communities*, May 22. www.pewsocialtrends.org/2018/05/22/demo graphic-and-economic-trends-in-urban-suburban-and-rural-communities/

Pianta, R. C., & Walsh, D. J. (1996). *High-Risk Children in Schools*. New York: Routledge.

Prilleltensky, I., Nelson, G., & Peirson, L. (2001). The role of power and control in children's lives: An ecological analysis of pathways toward wellness, resilience and problems. *Journal of Community and Applied Social Psychology, 11*, 143–158.

Probst, J. C., Barker, J. C., Enders, A. et al. (2018). Current state of child health in rural America: How context shapes children's health. *Journal of Rural Health, 34*, s3–s12.

Provasnik, S., KewalRamani, A., Coleman, M. M. et al. (2007). *Status of Education in Rural America* (NCES 2007–040). Washington, DC: National Center for Education Statistics, Institute of Education Sciences, US Department of Education.

Przybylski, A. K., & Weinstein, N. (2012). Can you connect with me now? How the presence of mobile communication technology influences face-to-face conversation quality. *Journal of Social and Personal Relationships, 30*, 1–10.

Radke-Yarrow, M., & Sherman, T. L. (1990). Hard growing: Children who survive. In J. Rolf, A. S. Masten, D. Cicchetti, et al. (Eds.) *Risk and Protective Factors in the Development of Psychopathology* (pp. 97–119). Cambridge: Cambridge University Press.

Radley, D. C., & Schoen, C. (2012). Geographic variation in access to care: The relationship with quality. *The New England Journal of Medicine, 367*, 3–6.

Raines, D. A., & Robinson, J. (2020). Format of parent education material preferred by new mothers. *Clinical Nursing Research, 29*, 256–259.

Raising Children Network. (2020). *Community Connections for Children: Friends, Neighbors and Local Organizations*. https://raisingchildren.net.au/ school-age/connecting-communicating/connecting/helping-your-child-con nect-with-others

Ramirez, S. M., & Villarejo, D. (2012). Poverty, housing, and the rural slum. *American Journal of Public Health, 102*, 1664–1675.

Rasmussen, M., Krolner, R., Klepp, K. I. et al. (2006). Determinants of fruit and vegetable consumption among children and adolescents: a review of the literature. Part I: Quantitative studies. *International Journal of Behavioral Nutrition and Physical Activity, 3*, 22.

Raymond, C. M., Kytta, M., & Stedman, R. (2017). Sense of place, fast and slow: The potential contributions of affordance theory to sense of place. *Frontiers in Psychology*, *8*, 1674.

Regalado, M., & Halfon, N. (2001). Primary care services promoting optimal child development from birth to age 3 years: Review of the literature. *Archives of Pediatrics and Adolescent Medicine*, *155*, 1311–1322.

Real, B., & Rose, R. N. (2017). Rural Libraries in the United States. American Library Association Report, July. www.ala.org/advocacy/sites/ala.org.advo cacy/files/content/pdfs/Rural%20paper%2007-31-2017.pdf

Regecova, V., & Kellcrova, E. (1995). Effects of urban noise pollution on blood pressure and heart rate in school children. *Journal of Hypertension*, *13*, 405–412.

Reisig, M. D., & Cancino, J. M. (2004). Incivilities in nonmetropolitan communities: The effects of structural constraints, social conditions, and crime. *Journal of Criminal Justice*, *32*, 15–29.

Repetti, R. L., Robles, T. F., & Reynolds, B. (2011). Allostatic processes in the family. *Development and Psychopathology*, *23*, 921–938.

Reupert, A. E., Maybery, D. J., & Kowalenko, N. M. (2012). Children whose parents have mental illness: Prevalence, need and treatment. *Medical Journal of Australia Open*, *1* (Suppl. 1), 7–9.

Rice, V. H. (2012). Theories of stress and its relationship to health. In V. H. Rice (Ed.), *Handbook of Stress, Coping and Health: Implications for Nursing Research, Theory, and Practice* (2nd ed., pp. 22–42). Thousand Oaks, CA: Sage.

Richman, A. L., Miller, P. M., & LeVine, R. A. (1988). Cultural and educational variations in maternal responsiveness. *Developmental Psychology*, *28*, 614–621.

Richert, R. A., Robb, M. B., Fender, J. G. et al. (2010). Word learning from baby videos. *Archives of Pediatrics and Adolescent Medicine*, *164*, 432–437.

Rideout, V. (2017). *The Common Sense Census: Media Use by Kids Age Zero to Eight*. San Francisco, CA: Common Sense Media.

Rideout, V., Hamel, E., & Kaiser Family Foundation. (2006). *The Media Family: Electronic Media in the Lives of Infants, toddlers, Preschoolers and Their Parents*. Menlo Park, CA: Kaiser Family Foundation

Rideout, V., & Katz, V. S. (2016). *Opportunity for All? Technology and Learning in Low-income Families*. Families and Media Project Report, The Joan Ganz Cooney Center at Sesame Workshop, New York. www .joanganzcooneycenter.org/wp-content/uploads/2016/01/jgcc_opportunity forall.pdf

Ritchie, H., & Roser, M. (2019a). *Access to Energy*. Our World in Data, November. https://ourworldindata.org/energy-access

Ritchie, H., & Roser, M. (2019b). *Urbanization*. Our World in Data, November. https://ourworldindata.org/urbanization

Rivara, F. P., & Mueller, B. A. (1987). The epidemiology and causes of childhood injuries. *Journal of Social Issues*, *43*, 13–31.

Rivas, I., Basagana, X., Cirach, M. et al. (2019). Association between early life exposure to air pollution and working memory and attention. *Environmental Health Perspectives*, *127*, 3169.

Roberts, D., Foehr, U., & Rideout, V. (2005). *Generation M: Media in the Lives of 8–18-Year-Olds*. Menlo Park, CA: Kaiser Family Foundation.

Robinson, S., & Fall, C. (2012). Infant nutrition and later health: A review of current evidence. *Nutrients*, *8*, 859–874.

Roche, K. M., & Ghazarian, S. R. (2012). The value of family routines for academic success of vulnerable children. *Journal of Family Issues*, *33*, 874–897.

Roe, J. J., Thompson, C. W., Aspinall, P. A. et al. (2013). Green space and stress: Evidence from cortisol measures in deprived urban communities. *International Journal of Environmental Research and Public Health*, *10*, 4086–4103.

Rogoff, B., & Morelli, G. (1989). Perspectives on children's development from cultural psychology. *American Psychologist*, *44*, 343–348.

Rohner, R. P., Khaleque, A., & Cournoyer, D. E. (2005). Parental acceptance-rejection: Theory, methods, cross-cultural evidence, and implications. *Ethos*, *33*, 299–334.

Rollings, K A., Wells, N. M., Evans, G. W. et al. (2017). Housing and neighborhood physical quality: Children's mental health and motivation. *Journal of Environmental Psychology*, *50*, 17–23,

Romanowicz, M., Vande Voort, J. L., Shekunov J. et al. (2019). The effects of parental opioid use on the parent-child relationship and children's developmental and behavioral outcomes: A systematic review of published reports. *Child and Adolescent Psychiatry and Mental Health*, 13, 5.

Rosales, F. J., Reznick, J. S., & Zeisel, S. H. (2009). Understanding the role of nutrition in brain and behavioral development of toddlers and preschool children: Identifying and overcoming methodological barriers. *Nutrition Neuroscience*, *12*, 190–202.

Roser, M., Ortiz-Ospina, E., & Ritchie, H. (2019). *Life Expectancy*. Our World in Data, October. https://ourworldindata.org/life-expectancy

Ross, E. J., Graham, D. L., Money, K. M. et al. (2015). Developmental consequences of fetal exposure to drugs: What we know and what we still must learn. *Neuropsychopharmacology Reviews*, *40*, 61–87.

Rossiter, J. (2017). Robotics, smart materials, and their future impact for humans. *MIT Technology Review*, April 6. www.technologyreview.com/s/604097/robotics-smart-materials-and-their-future-impact-for-humans/

Roy, A. I., McCoy, D. C., & Raver, C. C. (2014). Instability versus quality: Residential mobility, neighborhood poverty, and children's self-regulation. *Developmental Psychology, 50*, 1891–1896.

Rubio-Codina, M., Attanasio, O, & Grantham-McGregor, S. (2016). Mediating pathways in the socio-economic gradient of child development: Evidence from children 6–42 months in Bogota. *International Journal of Behavioral Development, 40*, 483–491

Ruiz-Casares, M., Nazif-Munoz, J. I., Iwo, R. et al. (2018). Nonadult supervision of children in low- and middle-income countries: Results from 61 national population-based surveys. *International Journal of Environmental Research and Public Health, 15*, 1564.

Runyan, D., Hunter, W., Socolar, R. et al. (1998). Children who prosper in unfavorable circumstances: The relationship to social capital. *Pediatrics, 101*, 12–18.

Runyan, M. K., Faust, J., & Orvaschel, H. (2002). Differential symptom patterns of post-traumatic stress disorder (PTSD) in maltreated children with and without depression. *Child Abuse and Neglect, 26*, 39–53.

Ryan R. M., & Claessens, A. (2013). Associations between family structure changes and children's behavior problems: The moderating effects of timing and marital birth. *Developmental Psychology, 49*, 1219–1231.

Ryan, R. M., & Deci, E. L. (2017). *Self-Determination Theory: Basic Psychological Needs in Motivation, Development, and Wellness.* New York: Guilford Press.

Saelens, B. E., Glanz, K., Frank, L. D. et al. (2018). Two-year changes in child weight status, diet, and activity by neighborhood nutrition and physical activity environment. *Obesity, 26*, 1338–1346.

Salmon, J., Timperio, A., Carver, A. et al. (2005). Association of family environment with children's television viewing and low level of physical activity. *Obesity Research, 13*, 1939–1951.

Sammons, P., Toth, K., Sylve, K. et al. (2015), The long-term role of the home learning environment in shaping students' academic attainment in secondary school. *Journal of Children's Services, 10*, 189–201.

Sandstrom, H., & Huerta. J. (2013). *The Negative Effects of Instability on Child Development: A Research Synthesis.* Urban Institute, Low Income Working Families, Discussion Paper No. 3. www.urban.org/sites/default/files/publication/32706/412899-The-Negative-Effects-of-Instability-on-Child-Development-A-Research-Synthesis.PDF

Sansour, K., Sheridan, M., Jutte, D. et al. (2011). Family socioeconomic status and child executive functions: The roles of language, home environment, and single parenthood. *Journal of the International Neuropsychological Society, 17*, 120–132.

Scales, P., & Leffert, N. (1999). *Developmental Assets*. Minneapolis, MN: Search Institute.

Scannell, L., &. Gifford, R. (2017). The experienced psychological benefits of place attachment. *Journal of Environmental Psychology, 51*, 256–269.

Scarr, S., & McCartney, K. (1983). How people make their own environments: A theory of genotype great than environment effects. *Child Development, 54*, 424–435.

Schmidt. M., & Vandewater, E. (2008). Media and attention, cognition, and school achievement. *The Future of Children, 18*, 63–86.

Schooler, C. (1999). The workplace environment: Measurement, psychological effects, and basic issues. In S. L. Friedman & T. D. Wachs (Eds.), *Measuring Environment Across the Life Span* (pp. 229–248). Washington, DC: American Psychological Association.

Seltzer, J. A. (2019). Family change and changing family demography. *Demography, 56*, 405–425.

Semansky, R., Willging, C., Ley, D. J. et al. (2012). Lost in the rush to national reform: Recommendations to improve impact on behavioral health providers in rural areas. *Journal of Health Care for the Poor and Underserved, 23*, 842–856.

Semple, S., Strathdee, S., Zians, J. et al. (2001). Methamphetamine-using parents: The relationships between parental role strain and depressive symptoms. *Journal of Studies on Alcohol and Drugs, 72*, 954–964.

Senechal, M., & LeFevre, J. A. (2002). Parental involvement in the development of children's reading skill: A five-year longitudinal study. *Child Development, 73*, 445–460.

Sharkey, P., & Faber, J. W. (2014). Where, when, why, and for whom do residential contexts matter? moving away from the dichotomous understanding of neighborhood effects. *Annual Review of Sociology, 40*, 559–579.

Sheely, A. (2010). Work characteristics and family routines in low- wage families. *Journal of Sociology and Social Welfare, 37*, 59–77.

Shenoy, S., Desai, G., Venkatasubramanian, B. et al. (2019). Parenting in mothers with schizophrenia and its relation to facial emotion recognition deficits: A case control study. *Asian Journal of Psychiatry, 40*, 55–59.

Siegenthaler, E., Munder, T., & Egger, M. (2012). Effect of preventive interventions mentally ill parents on the mental health of the offspring: systematic review and meta-analysis. *Journal of the American Academy of Child and Adolescent Psychiatry, 51*, 8–17.

Simon, H. K., Tamura, T., & Colton, K. (2003). Reported level of supervision of young children while in the bathtub. *Ambulatory Pediatrics, 3,* 106–108.

Simpson-Adkins, G. J., & Daiches, A. (2018). How do children make sense of the parent's mental health difficulties: A meta-synthesis. *Journal of Child and Family Studies, 27,* 2705–2716.

Skinner, A. C., & Slifkin, R. T. (2007). Rural/urban differences in barriers to and burden of care for children with special health care needs. *The Journal of Rural Health, 23,* 150–157.

Smith, V. C., Wilson, C. R., & Committee on Substance Use and Prevention. (2016). Families affected by parental substance use. *Pediatrics, 138,* e20161575.

Solari, C., & Mare, R. (2012). Housing crowding effects on children's well being. *Social Science Research, 41,* 464–476.

Solis, J. M., Shadur, J. M., Burns, A. R. et al. (2012). Understanding diverse needs of children whose parents abuse substances. *Current Drug Abuse Review, 5,* 135–147.

Soto-Icaza, P., Aboitiz, F., & Billeke, P. (2015). Development of social skills in children: Neural and behavioral evidence for elaboration of cognitive models. *Frontiers in Neuroscience, 9,* 333.

Spagnola, M., & Fiese, B. H. (2007). Family routines and rituals, A context for development in the lives of young children. *Infants and Young Children, 20,* 284–299.

Sparks, S. (2016). Student mobility: How it affects learning. *Education Week,* August 11. www.edweek.org/ew/issues/student-mobility/

Stace, S., & Roker, D. (2005). *Parental Supervision: The Views and Experiences of Young People and Their Parents.* Joseph Rowntree Foundation Report. www.jrf.org.uk/report/parental-supervision-views-and-experiences-young-people-and-their-parents

Stack, R. J., & Meredith, A. (2018). The impact of financial hardship on single parents: An exploration of the journal from social distress to seeking help. *Journal of Family and Economic Issues, 39,* 233–2452.

Stamps, A. (2004). Mystery, complexity, legibility and coherence: A meta-analysis. *Journal of Environmental Psychology, 24,* 1–16.

Stansfeld, S., & Clark, C. (2015). Health effects of noise exposure in children. *Current Environmental Health Report, 2,* 171–178.

Strasburger, V. C., Jordan, A. M., & Donnerstein, E. (2012). Children, adolescents, and the media: Health effects. *Pediatric Clinics of North America, 59,* 533–587.

Strasser, R. (2003). Rural health around the world: Challenges and solutions. *Family Practice, 20,* 457–463.

Stright, A. D., Herr, M. Y., & Neitzel, C. (2009). Maternal scaffolding of children's problem solving and children's adjustment in kindergarten: Hmong families in the United States. *Journal of Educational Psychology*, *101*, 207–218.

Suarez-Orozco, C., & Suarez-Orozco, M. M. (2001). *The Developing Child: Children of Immigration*. Cambridge, MA: Harvard University Press.

Substance Abuse & Mental Health Services Administration. (2019). *Key Substance Use and Mental Health Indicators in the United States: Results from the 2018 National Survey on Drug Use and Health* (HHS Publication No. PEP19-5068, NSDUH Series H-54). Rockville, MD: Center for Behavioral Health Statistics and Quality, Substance Abuse and Mental Health Services Administration. www.samhsa.gov/data/sites/default/files/cbhsq-reports/NSDUHNationalFindingsReport2018/NSDUHNationalFindingsReport2018.pdf

Suglia, S., Duarte, C., Sandel, M. et al. (2010). Social and environmental stressors in the home and childhood asthma. *Journal of Epidemiology and Community Health*, *64*, 636–642.

Suk, W. A., Ahanchian, H., Asante, K. A. et al. (2016). Environmental pollution: An under-recognized threat to children's health, especially in low- and middle-income countries. *Environmental Health Perspectives*, *124*, A41–A45.

Sun, J., Liu, Y., Chen, E. E. et al. (2016). Factors related to parents' engagement in cognitive and socio-emotional caregiving in developing countries: Results from the Multiple Indicators Cluster Survey 3. *Early Childhood Research Quarterly*, *36*, 21–31.

Swan, D. W., Grimes, J., & Owens, T. (2013). The *State of Small and Rural Libraries in the United States* (Research Brief series, no. 5; IMLS-2013-RB -05). Washington, DC: Institute of Museum and Library Services.

Tabor, K. M., Smith, T. S., Brown, M. et al. (2018). Presynaptic inhibition selectively gates auditory transmission to the brainstem startle circuit. *Current Biology*, *28*, 2527–2535.

Takeuchi, L. (2011). *Families Matter: Designing Media for a Digital Age*. New York: The Joan Ganz Cooney Center at Sesame Workshop. www.joanganzcooneycenter.org/wp-content/uploads/2011/06/jgcc_familiesmatter.pdf

Taylor, Z. E., Conger, R. D., Robins, R. W. et al. (2015). Parenting practices and perceived social support; Longitudinal relations with the social competence of Mexican-origin children. *Journal of Latino Psychology*, *3*, 193–208.

Thomas, L., & Kalucy, R. (2003). Parents with mental illness: Lacking motivation to parent. *International Journal of Mental Health Nursing*, *12*, 153–157.

Thornock, C. M., Nelson, L. J., Porter, C. L. et al. (2019). There is no place like home: The associations between residential attributes and family functioning. *Journal of Environmental Psychology, 64*, 39–47.

Tigges, L. M., Browne, I., & Green, G. P. (1998). Social isolation of the urban poor: Race, class, and neighborhood effects on social resources. *The Sociological Quarterly, 39*, 53–787.

Timperio, A., Salmon, J. Ball, K. et al. (2008). Family physical activity and sedentary environments and weight in children. *International Journal of Pediatric Obesity, 3*, 160–167.

Tomopoulos, S., Dreyer, B., Tamis-LeMonda, C. et al. (2006). Books, toys, parent-child interaction, and development in young Latino children. *Ambulatory Pediatrics, 6*, 72–78.

Trent, M., Dooley, D. G., Douge, J. et al. (2019). The impact of racism on child and adolescent health. *Pediatrics, 144*, e20191765.

Triguero-Mas, M., Dadvand, P., Cirach, M. et al. (2015). Natural outdoor environments and mental and physical health: Relationships and mechanisms. *Environment International, 77*, 35–41.

UNESCO. (2010). *Education for All, Global Monitoring Report – 2010. Reaching the Marginalized.* http://en.unesco.org/gem-report/report/2010/reaching-marginalized

UNICEF. (2019). *Progress on Drinking Water, Sanitation, and Hygiene 2000–2017, Special Focus on Inequalities*, Report, June. www.unicef.org/reports/progress-on-drinking-water-sanitation-and-hygiene-2019

UNICEF. (2020). *UNICEF's Mission Statement*, March. www.unicef.org/about/who/index_mission.html

United Nations. (2019). *World Urbanization Prospects 2018: Highlights* (ST/ESA/SER.A/421). Department of Economic and Social Affairs, Population Division.

United Nations Development Program. (2014). *Human Development Report 2014. Sustaining Human Progress: Reducing Vulnerabilities and Building Resilience.* http://hdr.undp.org/sites/default/files/2015_human_development_report.pdf

United Nations Economic Commission for Africa. (2016). *Social Cohesion in Eastern Africa.* www.uneca.org/publications/social-cohesion-eastern-africa

US Department of Health and Human Services. (2015). *Child Health USA 2014.* http://mccb.hrsa.gov/chusa14/

US Department of Health and Human Services. (2017). *National Healthcare Quality and Disparities Report Chartbook on Rural Health Care.* AHRQ Publication No. 17(18)-001-2-EF, October. www.ahrq.gov/sites/default/files/wysiwyg/research/findings/nhqrdr/chartbooks/qdr-ruralhealthchartbook-update.pdf

US Department of Health and Human Services. (2019). *Child Maltreatment 2017*. Children's Bureau Report, Administration for Children and Families. www.acf.hhs.gov/cb/research-data-technology/statistics-research/child-maltreatment

Valentine, G. (1997). A safe place to grow up? Parenting, perceptions of children's safety and the rural idyll. *Journal of Rural Studies*, *13*, 137–148.

Van Acker. K., & Vanbeselaere N. (2012). Heritage culture maintenance precludes host culture adoption and vice versa: Flemings' perceptions of Turks acculturation behavior. *Group Processes and International Relations*, *15*, 133–145.

van den Boom, D. C. (1994). The influence of temperament and mothering on attachment and exploration: An experimental manipulation of sensitive responsiveness among lower-class mothers with irritable infants. *Child Development*, *65*, 1457–1477.

Vandewater, E., & Lee, S-J. (2009). Measuring children's media use in the digital age: Issues and challenges. *American Behavioral Scientist*, *52*, 1152–1176.

van Fleet, J., Watkins, K., & Greubel, L. (2012). *Africa Learning Barometer*, September. www.brookings.edu/interactives/africa-learning-barometer/

Vernon-Feagans, L., Garrett-Peters, P., Willoughby, M. et al. (2012). Chaos, poverty, and parenting: Predictors of early language development. *Early Childhood Research Quarterly*, *27*, 339–351.

Vieno, A., Nation, M., Perkins, D. D. et al. (2010). Social capital, safety concerns, parenting, and early adolescents' antisocial behavior. *Journal of Community Psychology*, *38*, 314–328.

Villegas, A. (2013). The influence of technology on family dynamics. *Proceedings of the New York State Communication Association*, 2012. http://docs.rwu.edu/nyscaproceedings/vol2012/iss1/10

Von Bertalanffy, L. (1968). *General Systems Theory: Foundations, Development, Applications*. New York: George Braziller.

Wachs, T. D. (2000). *Necessary but Not Sufficient*. Washington, DC: American Psychological Association.

Walker, S. P., Wachs, T. D., Gardner, J. M. et al. (2007). Child development: Risk factors for adverse outcomes in developing countries. *Lancet*, *369*, 145–167.

Wallerstein, J., & Lewis, J. (2007). Disparate parenting and step-parenting with siblings in the post-divorce family: Report from a 10-year longitudinal study. *Journal of Family Studies*, *13*, 224–235.

Walsh, W. B., Craik, K. H., & Price, R. H. (2000). *Person-Environment Psychology: New Directions and Perspectives* (2nd ed.). New York: Routledge.

Wang, M., Aaron, C. P., Madrigano, J. et al. (2019). Association between long-term exposure to ambient air pollution and change in quantitatively assessed emphysema and lung function. *JAMA, 322,* 546–556.

Warschauer, M., & Matuchniak, T. (2010). New technology and digital worlds: Analyzing evidence of equity in access, use, and outcomes. *Review of Research in Education, 34,* 179–225.

Wartella, E., Huston, A, Rideout, V. et al. (2009). Studying media methods on children, Improving methods and measures. *American Behavioral Scientist, 52,* 1111–1114.

Wathen, C. N., & MacMillan, H. L. (2013). Children's exposure to intimate partner violence: Impacts and interventions. *Paediatric Child Health, 18,* 419–422.

Watters, C. (2008). *Refugee Children: Towards the Next Horizon.* New York: Routledge.

Waylen, A., & McKenna, F. (2009). The role of parental attitudes and monitoring in the risk exposure of young children. *Journal of Applied Social Psychology, 39,* 791–803.

Wedge, M. (2014). Overscheduled kids. How much of a good thing is too much? *Psychology Today,* August 16. www.psychologytoday.com/us/blog/suffer-the-children/201408/overscheduled-kids

Weisner, T. S. (2002). Ecocultural understandings of children's developmental pathways. *Human Development, 45,* 275–281.

Wells, N. M., & Harris, J. D. (2007). Housing quality, psychological distress, and the mediating role of social withdrawal: A longitudinal study of low-income women. *Journal of Environmental Psychology, 27,* 69–78.

Wells, M., Morrongiello, B. A., & Kane, A. (2012). Unintentional injury risk in school-age children: Examining interrelations between parent and child factors. *Journal of Applied Developmental Psychology, 33,* 189–196.

Whaley, A. L. (2000). Sociocultural differences in the developmental consequences of the use of physical discipline during childhood for African Americans. *Cultural Diversity and Ethnic Minority Psychology, 6,* 5–12.

Wheeler, B. W., Cooper, A. R., Page, A. S. et al. (2010). Greenspace and children's physical activity: A GPS/GIS analysis of the PEACH project. *Preventive Medicine, 51,* 148–152

White, M. P., Alcock, I., Wheeler, B. W. et al. (2013). Would you be happier living in a greener urban area? A fixed-effects analysis of panel data. *Psychological Science, 24,* 920–928.

Whiteside-Mansell, L., Bradley, R., McKelvey, L. et al. (2009). Parenting: Linking impacts of interpartner conflict to preschool children's social behavior. *Journal of Pediatric Nursing, 24,* 389–400.

Whiting, B., & Edwards, C. (1988). *Children of Different Worlds: The Formation of Social Behavior.* Cambridge, MA: Harvard University Press.

WHO (World Health Organization). (2018). *WHO Housing and Health Guidelines.* Geneva: WHO.

WHO (World Health Organization). (2019). *Drinking-Water.* Factsheet, June. www.who.int/news-room/fact-sheets/detail/drinking-water

Wilson, B. (2008). Media and children's aggression, fear, and altruism. *The Future of Children, 18,* 87–118.

Wilson, S., & Durbin, C. E. (2010). Effects of paternal depression on fathers' parenting behaviors: A meta-analytic review. *Clinical Psychological Review, 30,* 167–180.

Wlodarczyk, O., Schwarze, M., Rumpf. H. et al. (2017). Protective mental health factors in children of parents with alcohol and drug use disorders: A systematic review. *PLoS ONE, 12,* e179140.

Wolfgang, C. H., Stannard, L. L., & Jones, I. (2003). Early child development and care: Advanced constructional play with LEGOs among preschoolers as a predictor of later school achievement in mathematics. *Early Child Development and Care, 173,* 467–475.

Wong, B. B., & Candolin, U. (2015). Behavioral responses to changing environments. *Behavioral Ecology, 26,* 665–673.

Woodberry, A. E. (2017). Museums and rural schools. *Tufts Museum Studies* (blog.), April 5. http://sites.tufts.edu/museumstudents/2017/04/05/rural-museums-and-k-12-education/

Yeoh, S. L., Eastwood, J., Wright, I. M. et al. (2019). Cognitive and motor outcomes of children with prenatal opioid exposure. *JAMA Network Open, 2,* e197025.

Yeung, W., Linver, M. R., & Brooks-Gunn, J. (2002). How money matters for young children's development: Parental investment and family processes. *Child Development, 73,* 1861–1879.

Yildiz, B. M., Sasanguie, D., De Smedt, B. et al. (2018). Frequency of home numeracy activities is differentially related to basic number processing and calculation skills in kindergartners. *Frontiers in Psychology, 9,* 340.

Yongsi, N., Delali, H. B., & Dovie, B. K. (2007). Diarrheal diseases in the history of public health. *Archives of Medical Research, 38,* 159–163.

You, D., & Anthony, D. (2012). *Generation 2025: The Critical Importance of Understanding Demographic Trends for the Children of the 21st Century.* UNICEF Occasional Paper No. 1, September.

Zaltauske, V., & Petrauskiene, A. (2016). Associations between built environment and physical activity of 7–8-year-old children. Cross-sectional results from the Lithuanian COSI study. *Medicina (Kaunas)*, *52*, 366–371.

Zeitlin, M. (1996). My child is my crown: Yoruba parental theories and practices in early childhood. In S. Harkness & C. Super (Eds.), *Parents' Cultural Belief Systems* (pp. 407–427). New York: Guilford Press.

Zhang, D., Li, X., & Xue, J. (2015). Education inequality between rural and urban areas of the Peoples' Republic of China: Migrants' children education, and some implications. *Asian Development Review, 32*, 196–224.

Zimmerman, B. J. (2000). Attaining self-regulation: A social cognitive perspective. In M. Boekaerts, M. Zeidner, & P. R. Pintrich (Eds.), *Handbook of Self-Regulation* (pp. 13–39). San Diego, CA: Academic Press.

Zolkoski, S. M., & Bullock, L. M. (2012). Resilience in children and youth: A review. *Children and Youth Services Review, 34*, 2295–2303.

Zucker, R. A., Donovan, J. E., Masten, A. S. et al. (2009). Developmental processes and mechanisms: Ages 0–10. *Alcohol Research and Health, 32*, 16–29.

Cambridge Elements ≡

Child Development

Marc H. Bornstein

National Institute of Child Health and Human Development, Bethesda
Institute for Fiscal Studies, London
UNICEF, New York City

Marc H. Bornstein is an Affiliate of the *Eunice Kennedy Shriver* National Institute of Child Health and Human Development, an International Research Fellow at the Institute for Fiscal Studies (London), and UNICEF Senior Advisor for Research for ECD Parenting Programmes. Bornstein is President Emeritus of the Society for Research in Child Development, Editor Emeritus of *Child Development*, and founding Editor of *Parenting: Science and Practice.*

About the Series

Child development is a lively and engaging, yet serious and purposeful subject of academic study that encompasses myriad of theories, methods, substantive areas, and applied concerns. Cambridge Elements in Child Development proposes to address all these key areas, with unique, comprehensive, and state-of-the-art treatments, introducing readers to the primary currents of research and to original perspectives on, or contributions to, principal issues and domains in the field.

Cambridge Elements ☰

Child Development

Printed in the United States
By Bookmasters